Frontal Matter:
Glue Gone Wild

By Suzanne Samples

Edited by Barbara Lockwood

Text copyright © 2018 Running Wild Press
All rights reserved.

Published in North America and Europe by Running Wild Press. Visit Running
Wild Press at www.runningwildpress.com.

Educators, librarians, book clubs (as well as the eternally curious), go to
www.runningwildpress.com for teaching tools.

ISBN 978-1-947041-24-0 (pbk)
ISBN 978-1-947041-25-7 (ebook)
Library of Congress Control Number: 2018959806

Printed in the United States of America.

for Sarah and Dottie Biscotti, only one of which is real

You wanna see what's in my head?
Check it out 'cause,
I got pictures of what's in my head
—Ben Folds, native to The Dash

We are unusual and tragic and alive.
—Dave Eggers

And we all know how this will end.
—Sufjan Stevens

boone, north carolina

There is nothing special about living, but there is everything special about dying.

I do not know, not yet, that I will discover the very gifts death has to offer: tea, word search books, stuffed animals, a lot of socks.

A lot, a lot of socks.

I touch my head.

I am a terrible Victorianist.

I completed my Ph.D. the year I turned 31 and only read Victorian literature again when I finally assigned some Tennyson for a survey World Lit course.

I did not, to the chagrin of my wonderfully intelligent and encouraging major professor (who sent me a lovely care package with an adorable cat mug), attempt any scholarly articles or conference proceedings detailing and analyzing the Crimean War, *Desire and Domestic Fiction*, or Satis House from *Great Expectations*.

I was the worst.

I touch my head again.

I feel for the intuitive reasoning, the reflective capabilities, the faculties.

I press above my left eye.

I feel for the locality, the reasoning, the planning.

I manipulate the skin around my skull.

I wonder if phrenology was not a pseudoscience after all.

I tap my cranium.

I push.

I search for any foreign objects that may diminish my agreeableness, my intuition.

There is something there. There is something new, something that does not belong.

I do not know this yet, but I have a grade IV glioblastoma: terminal brain cancer.

I don't feel sick I don't feel sick I don't feel sick.

the cut

boone, north carolina

There is a chance I will write this and I will live.

There is a greater chance I will write this and I will die a few months later.

I have a grade IV glioblastoma in the left frontal lobe of my brain.

Brain. Fucking. Cancer.

I have accepted this, maybe. I have understood this, potentially. I have sucked my secrets onto these pages and given you a glimpse at my surprise brain cancer, my likely end.

Something random about me: I really like keys.

Something about brain cancer in the frontal lobe: it causes attention span problems.

I also really like commas in compound sentences, but sometimes I refuse to use them for some sort of dramatic effect. I have no idea how my writing professors would feel about this, although many of them sent me lovely cards and well wishes while I was sequestered in the sick, sterile hospital for about a month.

During Christmas and New Year's, of all times.

I am fucked.

I am so fucked.

I was fine.

Healthy.

Christmas presents loaded in my car, ready to be joined by me and my pets for a six-hour ride to West Virginia for the holidays.

Everything was fine.

And then everything went to shit within twenty minutes.

Everything.

Some coffee, a seizure, a CT scan, an emergency room doctor whispering *there is a mass on your brain. We don't know what it is yet. You're being transported to Winston-Salem immediately.*

He was holding my hand, and I was screaming. Crying. Panicked. Screaming *fuck* oh my god *fuck.*

I did not cry again until I fell on the dingy blue bathroom floor of the neurology unit when I was supposed to be asleep after my craniotomy.

Troublemaker, free spirit, rogue.

There is a chance I will write this and I will live and piss off everyone who reads these words.

In a way, a terminal diagnosis of brain cancer in my left frontal lobe means I just don't care about pleasing people anymore. Like Plath in "Tulips," there is a simultaneous emptiness and freedom that allows me to feel as if I can say anything, do anything, and no one can prevent me from showing my soul, just like I exposed my brain, my innermost parts, to that neurosurgery team in Winston-Salem.

Winston-Salem, North Carolina.

Sometimes people call it *The Dash*.

I learn this, bored one night before surgery, in my room at the neuro unit.

It should actually be a hyphen—Wikipedia notes this.

If I live: there is a chance my friends and family might hate me for these words. There is a greater chance, I hope, that they will understand how *honest writing is good writing*.

This is the phrase I preach to my students more than any other.

Honest writing is good writing.

The reverse works as well.

Good writing is honest writing.

I have to do this, I have to write this, I have to tell everyone.

Please take this key, unlock my ear, and twist.

I am still here.

I am still waiting.

I am still writing

I am still alive, right now.

boone, north carolina, hatchet coffee

Feeney and I had a misunderstanding.

Feeney: my friend, my gym buddy, my confidant.

I met Feeney through my roller derby team. Her quiet confidence, her genius in the kitchen, her willingness to help anyone in need, her terrible dad jokes, and her uncanny ability to react in medical emergencies that made me smile and feel safe in her presence. My other teammates and I joked that her shoulders were so ripped they deserved their own Facebook page. Feeney and I were teammates, friends, and single women with dogs who did not enjoy minding us or listening to our commands. We went to the gym together, enjoyed finding good food in Boone, and had deep conversations about how our love lives were *complete shit but we weren't quite that old yet so maybe, just maybe, there was still hope.*

But something went awry, something went weird.

I hurt her because I said something I shouldn't have, let my awkwardness take over when I should have stayed quiet and let the moment pass like just another gust of wind down Boone, North Carolina's King Street during that record cold December.

My questions now: can I blame that moment on my frontal lobe? Or did I just make a mistake? What do you think, my new friend, my tumor? Did you play a part in this relationship mishap, or was that all SZ, all me?

I missed Feeney while we weren't communicating.

You probably missed her, too.

I planned to leave town and visit my parents on December 18th: Feeney's birthday. The night before, I panicked after dinner. I wanted to glue my loose ends together before leaving town, and there were so many. I could fix this misunderstanding with Feeney, if only I could release my stubbornness and just say *I'm so sorry for being an asshole.* I knew she would forgive me because she was Feeney. She was sweet and considerate.

I knew she missed me as well. I knew she would want to get back to the gym, back to our lives, back to drinking coffee out of the Esteban the Elephant mug at Melanie's, our favorite breakfast spot.

Hey, I texted her. *I'm sorry. I miss you.*

She wanted to talk the next morning before I left town. Early. Her birthday. The day final grades were due. I had all of my grades turned in except for three students who needed extra time to finish their writing portfolios, so I packed the night before and planned to finish the grades before she showed up at the coffee shop where we agreed to meet.

You were with me the whole time, tumor, but I had no idea.

I should have never felt lonely, never felt isolated or unloved.

When you and I show up to the coffee shop, tumor, we listen to a Bible study group discuss how Mary felt before delivering Jesus on Christmas Day. Naturally, I have so many issues with this—sure, I believe in Jesus, but there is no way he was actually born on December 25th, and I do not think for a moment that any of these Bible study people have a clue what Mary felt when schlepping around the supposed world savior through some poorly-lit-night-sky-desert- excursion.

But whatever.

There is one guy, a guy you and I call The Philosopher, who keeps yammering about how the words *witness* and *testimony* basically *mean the same thing, ya know* in Hebrew, but you and I have no reference for this. The Bible study group believes him but seems annoyed that he cares so much about two words when the other group members want to talk about *baby Jesus* and *nativities smelling of Carolina pines* and how *someone stole forty bucks* from one of the ladies earlier that morning.

Feeney and I work through our misunderstanding almost immediately.

You gave me no headaches, tumor.

No blurry vision.

The worst you did: presented me with a possessed leg that interrupts the shit out of that Bible study.

Our Father who art I think I have a Charlie horse *in heaven hallowed*

8

be thy name I don't understand why it's moving up my leg oh my god *thy kingdom come thy will be done* oh my god it won't stop moving up my leg *as earth as it is* Jesus Christ oh my god my entire side my arm my hip *in heaven amen.*

Feeney moves me to the floor near the sacks of coffee beans. I had a date here a month ago—was it a date? Something like that? And we sat on those bags of beans, our cheeks as flushed as the cranberry chai because we realized we shared the same therapist.

You, you fucking tumor, became the brain of my leg, the exorcist of my right side. You demon, you piece of shit.

The Bible study group abandoned the ark of the coffee shop when my leg started swinging like an unwieldy clock hand; they packed their flimsy reproductions of ancient texts, their mittens, their stories about porcelain-skinned baby Jesus, and left.

One guy—not The Philosopher but more of a casual Jesus observer—assists Feeney in dragging me to the car. A flood of worry, doubt, and fear clouds my own prayers, my own understanding of the future told by stars.

I do not touch my head.

I do not touch you.

watauga medical center, boone, north carolina
I am super-pleased with the stroke I have had.

The stroke I believe I have had.

There is a 20-minute space in the emergency room, a 20-minute reprieve before I find out about the mass in my brain. A 20-minute frame of reasoning where I have time to think. Time to consider. Time to believe.

Believe that because I have this strange seizure on the right side of my body, I have had a stroke. But just a little one. A small stroke, a brief annoyance. Nothing to really worry about.

I do not know much about strokes. My grandmother had one. She threw a bunch of receipts and papers around her office, made a huge mess, was in the hospital for a few days, and then was really angry with my mother for nine more years. My mom did not do anything wrong and helped my grandmother recover until the end of her life, but my grandmother never forgave her.

For what, we never knew.

So yeah, super-pleased with this little stroke of mine.

I am speaking, I am of clear mind, and I am making fun of how they made me take off my underwear to put on a hospital gown. I do not know, not at this time, that I will not put on regular underwear for another five days.

This is not to make light of a stroke; I know they can be devastating.

I know they can easily kill people or greatly decrease one's quality of life.

I simply believe I have gotten very lucky. Very, very lucky.

Of course I have had a stroke—people with type one diabetes, especially people who have had type one diabetes *for fucking ever* like I have, are highly susceptible to other types of health issues. So this makes sense. This fits into the plan. This resonates. I have had a stroke in my mid-30s because I have had type one for 31 years, and this is just. What. Happens.

My right side will come back. The emergency department doctors will give me some sort of medication, and I will be the same SZ (how I know myself), the same 9lb Hammer (how my roller derby team knows me), the same Dr. SZ (how my students know me) I have worked so hard to become.

I will learn to take better care of myself, check my blood sugar more frequently, and wear my insulin pump every single day.

I will not eat candy. I will not feel sick. I will not wake up in the middle of the night with high blood sugars because I fucked up my insulin pump infusion and did not check my levels before bed.

Do you think I had a stroke? I text my friend and derby teammate, Rolli. Rolli has worked in the medical field for so long that she basically knows as much as any doctor. She set her broken leg herself after a hockey stop went wrong at derby practice and caused her tibia and fibula to snap. Rolli knows things—Rolli knows everything.

I don't know, she says. *I don't know.*

She is worried. I can tell. She is worried that I did have a stroke, and this could be bad. Really bad. But I know, with all of the medical knowledge I don't have, that this had to be a stroke, a little mini stroke, and I am going to be fine. I am going to recover within a few days, maybe even a few hours, and everything will go back to normal. I will return to my apartment, tell my parents that I need another day to recover before I drive to see them, and spend time with my beloved pets.

I don't feel sick I don't feel sick I don't feel sick.

Easiest stroke ever.

Best case scenario.

When the emergency room doctor returns to tell me that *there is a mass in my brain*, and I will immediately be transported to Winston-Salem for *further treatment*, I scream. I heave. I hyperventilate.

I hold my teammate Jenna's hand and repeat *I can't do this I can't do this I can't do this. I'm not strong enough I'm not strong enough I'm not strong enough. They are going to put fucking staples in my head I just know it I just know it I just know it.*

She squeezes my hand and says *You are strong enough. You are.*

When Jenna steps out, I immediately call my mother.

It's probably an abscessed tooth, she says. *Didn't you say you were having tooth pain?*

I did not have a stroke.

I do not have an abscessed tooth.

I have a mass in my brain, and I am headed to Winston-Salem for an MRI, a craniotomy, and weeks, months, years of recovery and rehabilitation.

I am no longer super-pleased.

wake forest baptist hospital, emergency department, the dash
I put the $50 between my legs.

This seems like the safest place.

My ambulance driver, who happens to be my roller derby teammate's mother, gives me the cash and says *you're going to need this here.*

Prior to the transport, she fears I will vomit during the ride to Winston-Salem, but I do not; I feel better in the ambulance, as if I am observing the winter blues, greens, and yellows fade into the mountains forever, or at least until the next late afternoon.

The emergency department feels like a worn department store. Old pens litter half-cleaned tables. I see black creeping around a wall vent and wonder if its mold or discoloration. Employees yell at one another about vital signs and pilled sweaters.

I am alone.

Only for a few moments, but these moments make me feel very still, quiet, and frightened. I miss my cats. I miss my dog. I know I will not return home for at least a few days; I do not realize I will not return home for almost a month.

I put the $50 between my legs.

Make sure you do not have underwear on, they tell me. *You can't wear them for the MRI.*

I do not have underwear on.

I feel very, very naked and exposed.

At first, no one mentions the $50.

Cold hard cash.

Everything I have.

At this moment, I own nothing else. I am nothing else. I am here, and I am alive. I am waiting for the worst news, but I do not know yet that I will live here. I will remain. I will become something else than anything I have been before, someone completely different.

wake forest baptist hospital, holding unit, the dash

Who did this to you? A doctor asks before I receive my first official MRI. I do not know this doctor, and this is my first night as a patient in Wake Forest Baptist Hospital. I will never see this doctor again, and I have no idea what her title, specialty, or reason is.

I have waited seven hours for the MRI, and she is the first doctor I have seen.

She is worried—very worried—about my haircut.

Karrie at Haircut 101, I say.

No one here did this?

No.

I have completely shaved the left side of my head for two years. It is as if I predicted this would happen. It's as if I prepared myself for a craniotomy, years before this tumor made itself the demon of my right leg and my life.

My sister is a hairstylist in Brooklyn, and she suggested the haircut when I told her I was bored. *You have a lot of cowlicks on your left side,* she said. *Shaving it will make it easier to manage.*

And it was fun, asymmetric, different.

Naturally, whenever I attended big roller derby tournaments, my haircut matched about a fourth of the skaters in the venue. My students tended to like the *English professor with the weird haircut*, and the asymmetry became part of me, part of who I am.

Now I have worried the doctor.

This is your haircut?

Yes.

Oh god I thought someone here decided to prep you and just went for it.

Did I unknowingly prepare for you, tumor? Did I invite you in? Did I know that we would be living together for a short while before my leg went weak and I found myself in a bleakly gray hospital room with so many questions, questions, questions running through my supposedly sick brain?

I do not feel sick I do not feel sick I do not feel sick.

I do not feel like I am dying.

I am not yet sure if I am, how I am, when I am.

wake forest baptist hospital, the dash

During my first MRI, I stare at the technicians through the mirror that allows me to see just what they are up to.

And let me tell you, those technicians are up to things. They are working, sure, but they also look like they are having a pretty good time. Laughing with one another, joking about the poor cafeteria lunch choices, wondering how Tim and Marianne's date went last night.

Just another day at work.

Whenever I come close to drifting off, the warzone opens again. The MRI bullets buzz through my ears and hit the insides of the machine before ricocheting off the plastic and pulsing through my veins like the cold IV contrast that no warm blankets could ever ameliorate.

I cannot move, I cannot twitch.

What would happen if I did?

No one has told me.

I do not know if they could start where they left off, or if they would have to begin the process again. I do not know any of these things. I talk to students about topic sentences and occasionally, William Wordsworth. I do not know what happens, or what should happen, during an MRI.

Can the technicians see things? Can they recognize a tumor, even if they are not allowed to say anything? Do they sit in front of me and say to themselves *yikes, that poor girl! She looks so young and full of life. That tumor is fucking huge. Better her than one of us, eh?*

If I am not in a warzone, I am in a 1980s television set. Maybe a computer from 1998, an old Dell trying to use an AOL dialup connection. I am right in the middle, right between some wires, right around some electrical shocks and faulty fixtures. I can hear everything, experience everything, but I cannot stop the sounds, the magnetic fields, the firings of the machine.

Do you stop them, dear tumor?

When those magnetic fields hit you, do they cease their drone, their buzz, their noise?

I can see the MRI technicians laugh. I know they are not laughing at me, but I yearn to know what is so funny. A cat video? A new colleague who taught patients to tie their gowns on backward? A dad joke about non-stick socks? I feel so outside of everyone, everything.

Except the television, except the computer.

I am inside of the machine for at least another thirty minutes; I know this because I can feel the contrast leak into my veins and fill my body with a frigid unknown. The technicians told me this *would happen halfway through*, so I know I will hear more failed dialup connections, sense more magnetic fields attempting to move through my head until they stop at you, tumor.

You are the reason for everyone's, everything's failure.

I do not know what you mean yet.

At this point, you are still *just a mass*. I know nothing about your green, cancerous garbage cells. I do not know that you resemble a torn piece of monkey bread, a squirt of silly string. I just know that you are there, and you are waiting.

Waiting to kill me or waiting for the surgeon to wipe you out with a sterile tissue.

Or something like that.

I suppose we wait for one another, wait to see what happens next.

I don't feel sick I don't feel sick I don't feel sick.

wake forest baptist hospital, holding unit, the dash
Three months before *The Seizure that Changed Everything*, I played in my final roller derby bout.

I played roller derby for five competitive seasons.

I was never the best blocker, never the meanest one on the track, never the hardest hitter, but I did well. I was good. Good enough. I could stay low—thank you, short stature—I could be sneaky, and I could deliver a decent shoulder pop to the chest. I always did a nice job staying with my wall (the other blockers on the track from the same team), and I provided swift offense to my jammer, who was responsible for scoring the team's points.

Most people who knew me, especially those who grew up with me in my small, wholesome West Virginia hometown, found themselves surprised at my roller derby obsession. I did not play sports in high school—I was a competitive baton twirler, a sport in its own right, but I never joined a team or gave myself over to a group of people aiming toward a similar goal.

When a friend from graduate school convinced me to attend the first roller derby practice of the season, I found myself hooked like a tired jammer attempting to push her way through a tough wall.

Roller derby is what church should be, my mom observes when she arrives at the hospital a day later. *I mean church people say they are going to do things, and sometimes they do. Other times they don't. But roller derby teammates? They are there!*

My mom becomes an earnest roller derby fan after she sees my teammates give up their hours, their afternoons, their days to follow the ambulance to The Dash, to see me undergo my first MRI, to give up Christmas with their families to watch me recover from brain surgery. She begins to understand that teammates are not just responsible for one another on the track—they are responsible for one another during divorces, failed career paths, brain cancer. There is no vow, no notarized statement, just an unspoken rule that *whatever happens, your wall, your teammates, your jammers will be there.*

I do not know any other sport with quite the support system; despite derby's ultimate competitiveness, everyone cares, and everyone wants the best for their teammates, their competitors, and skaters from around the world whom they have never met.

JC is the only one with me on the first night who does not skate, but we adopt her as part of our team, part of our clan.

What the hell do you all do? my first nursing assistant asks. She says her name is *Shurry*. I ask her twice to be sure.

Shurry.

You all are like a brick shithouse softball team, Shurry says.

I have never heard this expression before, but I am not surprised that Shurry has noticed. Feeney's shoulders could have a softball team all their own.

I can't decide, though, if Shurry says this because we all seem muscular or because we all seem gay. Not all of us are, of course, but I have questions about that now and probably will until I finally die.

After dinner, I fall asleep.

I am skating with my typical wall of blockers, and the opposing jammer pushes on our backs with her bony shoulders. However, we stay together and puzzle our shapes into one another until we become a single, very wide person who takes up the entire track. The jammer cannot jut a single hip past us, and she remains stuck for the entire two minutes of the jam, my dream. My teammates and I speak to one another in calm, controlled voices that simultaneously soothe our blocking anxieties while causing the jammer to doubt the purpose of her life, the point of her existence.

When I see that my three teammates have fenced the opposing jammer, when I see that the opposing jammer pulls breaths in from the venue air as if she is dying on my cancer bed alongside me, I leave the wall and look to give offense, help my own jammer.

Ah, you should never leave a wall, I remember.

Unless you are sure, absolutely certain, that your teammates can cover the entire track without you.

I am certain, and I am right.

I sideswipe my body into the opposing wall, and my jammer notices. She sails past the opposing wall—who remain stymied from my unsuspecting hit—and becomes the initial jammer to exit the pack of skaters.

I do not feel sick I do not feel angry I do not feel as if I am dying.

I awake from the dream unsure as to whether or not we won our derby bout, but I know we did.

Brick shithouse softball team.

I know we did.

wake forest baptist hospital, neurology unit, the dash
Bailey brings me crackers and peanut butter.

I am not supposed to have them, but Bailey knows I am starving, will be starving, will regret not eating crackers and peanut butter by the next morning.

Bailey tells me he likes taking his girlfriend to Asheville when he has time off; Bailey and I both know there is something going on with him and Jason, his nursing assistant, but neither of us mention this.

I have been in the neurology unit since the MRI results confirmed the mass. I am casually waiting in my hospital bed for brain surgery, which will happen three days before Christmas, so I have had plenty of time to make these observations.

Bailey's girlfriend likes the fun socks people can buy at the weird store by the downtown coffee bus; she buys a pair during each trip they take, and then she and Bailey sip mocha lattes in the coffee bus and watch the tourists stroll down the street.

I am in no pain.

I cannot move my right side.

I am half a person, split down the middle, a tree trunk semi-rooted into the hospital bed.

You, my tumor, have stopped possessing my right leg for now. I had three more seizures in the hospital before they increased my medication to stop the shaking. You have given up, you little piece of shit. I know you, know your type. You stop by long enough to mess things up, and then you move on to something new, something more exciting.

You are a lot like my ex.

Now my right half just sits, watered by my catheter, waiting for some type of spark, an electrocution to liven me up again.

Bailey sits with me. He knows that although I can't stop smiling, I am terrified.

You left my face alone, tumor.

Thank you, thank you, thank you for that.

Jason comes in to talk about reality television. As I discover through some small talk, Jason's mother attended high school in West Virginia with my father and uncle. His mother texts him a yearbook photo later for confirmation. This makes me feel safer for some reason. Then, Jason and I discuss how the girl who won some singing competition looks exactly like another girl who won a different singing competition years ago.

Bailey laughs, smiles at Jason. If nothing else, their secretive relationship makes them a phenomenal nursing team, a pair who manages to make their patients feel less alone before craniotomies and anesthesia and head staples that bind together the details of brain surgery.

Do you like peanut butter, dearest tumor? It's one of my favorite foods. I will eat it straight from the jar, no problem.

Bailey puts the peanut butter on the cracker for me and stuffs the saltine into my mouth. This is nursing—feeding a patient peanut butter crackers because she cannot use her dominant hand, because she cannot make the plastic knife curve into the sterile peanut butter tub and spread the substance onto the cardboard cracker.

Sure, Bailey taped my IV minutes ago, sure he dragged me to the toilet and gave me ten seconds to take a piss on my own, sure he gave me a melatonin because he knew I would never sleep the night before surgery, sure—but he also made me feel human, made me feel as if I was getting a treat, made me feel as if I was not alone in those final few minutes before trying to fall asleep with the Wake Forest Baptist Hospital computer glaring into my face like a poorly written student paper.

Bailey takes care of me.

He tells me to *try and sleep*, to think about my cats and my writing and my books and my friends.

After everything ended in the neurology unit, I wondered about Bailey. About Jason. About their secret glances in the hallway, the spark of their hands when they passed off hospital bracelet scanners to one another, their slow blinks when no one was watching but me.

wake forest baptist hospital, neurology unit, the dash

My dad believes I am a carrot.

He is in his early 70s. He almost died last year when a tick bit him and gifted him with Lyme Disease. He had no initial signs, no symptoms.

Did semi-symptomless diseases run in the family? Perhaps.

Were my family members just annoyingly tough? Perhaps.

He was on a ventilator last Christmas and became a nursing home resident by New Year's. My mother advocated for him, made certain he received the best medical care. He was the nursing home Valentine King in February and was home by March.

He only uses the internet to browse guitars on Ebay.

My dad does not know how to use the internet for medical research. For most, I would say this is a positive, but for my dad, this means I cannot speak, respond, or verbalize my basic needs.

Because I have a brain tumor.

One we do not yet know is certainly most definitely assuredly brain cancer.

He thinks I am a radish.

My mom and I call him.

You can talk! You sound great! he says.

Yes. I sound great. I look great. I do not know how I should sound or look. The only other person I knew with brain cancer was my former high school principal. He looked pretty great himself until he died: he remained fit and stomped around the school to make certain all of the hippies put their hacky sacks in their JNCO pockets before third period began. I write this as a compliment to his character.

My father's relief smells like a mashed potato.

So comforting.

Neighbors and friends checking on my father say he looks as if he has aged ten years in these few days.

During another phone call, my dad tells me a story from my childhood. He bought a new bike to ride around town and decided to wash it with a water hose during a humid summer day. I pulled my own pink bike from the basement and told him I wanted to clean my bike, too.

Cleanin' my new bike, yes I am, yes I am.

He said I made up a three-minute song about the bike, which was neither new nor clean.

You were always just really creative, he says, as if I am already dead.

wake forest baptist hospital, neurology unit, the dash

Do you know who I am? a white-coated male asks me. He looks like an actor playing a doctor, maybe a new *Grey's Anatomy* resident, a little bit, but I know who he is. Or maybe I am hallucinating. No, I think, I am only on seizure medications, nothing that should make me hallucinate. Maybe a little bit. Do seizure medications make people hallucinate? Me hallucinate?

I have no idea.

Do you, tumor, make me see things? Everyone has asked about headaches, double vision. *Blurry things.* I had none of those, none of that.

I know exactly who this guy is.

I went to graduate school with Jon at Auburn University in Alabama. He and his wife Veronica began the program the year before I arrived, and they were both intelligent, kind, attractive people who seemed capable of either finding tenure-track jobs teaching literature and composition or traveling the world as spokespeople for a new flavored sparkling water.

Rarities who do not participate in Facebook or other social media indulgences, Jon and Veronica disappeared after graduation. I knew Jon had plans to attend medical school—he was simultaneously studying for oral comps and the MCAT, which drove the rest of us wild with wonder—but I had no idea he had followed through with his plan to graduate and then catapult himself beyond the vacuum of liberal arts and into the unknown of cells, medicine, and saving lives instead of reading about them.

I heard occasional updates about them from our mutual friend Amanda, but I assumed they'd returned to their home state of Arkansas to be closer to family and friends, had a couple children, and lived as paragons of perfection—but kind, admirable perfection—under the Midwestern starry skies.

Jon Lucas, I say. My voice sounds weak, uncertain, tired.

SZ. I saw your name assigned to my caseload and could not believe it.

Auburn, Alabama is exactly 427 miles, or roughly six-and-one-half hours from Wake Forest Baptist Hospital in Winston-Salem, North Carolina.

I do not know any other statistics or numbers, but I recognize—even in my semi-cognitive state of uncertainty, fear, and *whatthefuck*—that the odds of this happening have to be infinitesimal. It is unbelievable that an English graduate student finished his degree, completed another degree in medicine, and was then assigned to the case of a colleague who graduated from Auburn and moved to the tiny mountain town of Boone to teach English at Appalachian State University.

I still do not know if I believe in fate, ultimate destiny, God. A Milton class in undergrad really jumbled those ideas in my head, so I am still unsure. Could paradise be regained? A belief in fate, ultimate destiny, divine meeting?

I'm so happy to see you.

I don't have to be on your case—it's totally up to you.

Of course I want you on my case; you and Veronica were two of the smartest people at Auburn.

Jon smiles. I try to smile, but I am exhausted, curious as to why I somehow feel lucky.

wake forest baptist hospital, neurology unit, the dash

Chris visits me for thirty minutes in the neurology ward and brings me a stuffed orange cat and a plant that requires no water or sunlight.

Outside my family, Chris knows me better than anyone.

If anything happens to you, she says, *I will be at a level of zero functioning. Zero.*

This confuses me. Sure, we text daily. Sure, we have spent a lot of time around one another. Sure, we *have been through so much* together.

We began dating after Chris's brother passed away from an accidental fentanyl overdose. A couple weeks after beginning our relationship, I started puking and could not stop. Citing *diabetes complications*, I plopped in the hospital for a week. I puked bile. I vomited air. I dirtied so many gowns and pink kidney-shaped basins that I am certain the hospital charged me for over twenty of the plastic containers.

Chris undressed and dressed me in the hospital bathroom at least twelve times. The first time, after the ambulance brought me to the emergency room and after the doctors admitted me, Chris took off my dirty clothes and draped the striped gown over my exposed body. This was the first time Chris had seen me naked, but no one else knew this. Everyone assumed we already had stripped, fucked around, and paraded our bodies in front of one another in a show of confidence and potential love.

We had not.

Chris did a nice job of putting on my gown, did not expose me to herself or to the nurses, doctors, and patients' families bustling outside my fifth-floor room.

I never received a diagnosis, but Chris and I remained together for three years. We loved. We fought. We bought one another flowers and then halved those roses and marigolds with deadened scissors and butter knives. We destroyed. We created.

Chris has a new girlfriend now.

I feel badly that the new girlfriend must compete with me.

The Ex with the Brain Tumor that Will Later Be Deemed Terminal Brain Cancer.

No one can match that title; no one can reach that level of sorrow.

The new girlfriend seems nice. Stable. Unlikely to give Chris flowers and then destroy them an hour later after going through her phone and seeing texts to other ex-girlfriends. Ex-girlfriends without brain cancer. Ex-girlfriends who were just a general frustration instead of a threat to the relationship.

I hope the new girlfriend understands I am no threat; after all, I'm going to die. I am going to fucking die. Probably within a year. Maybe a few months. I will be a ghost to everyone's future relationships. Why? Because no one knows what might have happened with me. No one knows what I might have done, good or bad. No one knows if I would have become the love of their life or just another regretful few months, a few years where we would have both ended up hating one another and drinking red wine to ameliorate our self-imposed pain.

They will have to put me in a psych ward or something, Chris says. *You don't get it. We are close. I'm closer to you than I am with anyone else.*

Before this whole brain tumor thing happened, Chris never told me this. I suppose now is the time. I appreciated our post-relationship friendship, but I did not realize the weight of this friendship in our unstable present.

But you have a girlfriend. She will comfort you. She will make you happy. You don't get it. You really don't get it.

I suppose I do not. I do not *get it.* I've seen Chris move on; I've seen my obsessions, my loves move on from something that wasn't even officially there. I have watched everyone forget me and jump into other relationships, friendships, and pseudo-romances without giving *what we had* or *what we didn't have* a second thought.

There is nothing wrong with me. I am kind. I am talented, intelligent, and well spoken. I am, to some, even attractive. I have rarely met a person who has not complimented my smile or my *good spirit.* But things never worked out. Now I am likely to die without someone holding my hand, without someone petting my head and telling me how much I meant to them throughout my short life.

You have someone to help with these things, I say, a few more times. I think the more I say these words, the more their permanence will increase.

I will have to be institutionalized. Someone will have to lock me up.

You have a girlfriend, I say. *She will fix everything.*

As if that is her job, her assignment, her duty.

wake forest baptist hospital, neurology unit, the dash

I sign a stack of papers allowing my first cousin Emily to be my power of attorney.

We think the same, she says. *It's a good decision.*

Friends have signed up for shifts to care for my pets; I do not know about this until much later. My dog goes with my teammate Dollfin to her parents' house for Christmas. They all have red hair, so my pup looks like she biologically belongs to them.

A deacon comes into my room and asks if he can pray for me.

I let him.

wake forest baptist hospital, neurology unit, the dash

My surgeon looks about three years older than I am, and he has published multiple scholarly articles about brain tumors, Alzheimer's, and epilepsy. He speaks with the kindness of someone whose parents made certain he handled puppies carefully and opened doors for everyone, not just the elderly and those of the opposite sex. He is a ginger (with specks of gray) named Abrahm Bixton, and the balance of his name pleases me.

He resembles Van Gogh but looks more awake than pictures I have seen of the tired artist.

I read his scholarly articles before I fall asleep at night.

He operates on brains all day, and then he returns home to write about how those tumors affect peoples' memory, their mobility, their lives. He uses an elevated vocabulary and his own brain contains enough knowledge to rival Whitman's concept of self.

Dr. Bixton is Canadian, which should not matter, but it pleases me to think that he came all the way to North Carolina to pluck tumors out of peoples' brains.

Tumors like you, you little disaster.

Unlike you, tumor, Dr. Bixton makes me feel in control. He gives me options, choices.

He gives me the option of remaining awake throughout my surgery.

I try to imagine this.

I try to imagine him digging through my scalp and cracking open my skull to find you, my little hairball tumor. I try to imagine him listening to something like Vance Joy as he lifts you out with a scalpel and lifts

26

you toward the light like a scavenger hunt prize.

Oh no, no thank you, I say.

Being awake during the surgery would allow us to ask you to do things like try to move your leg while we work, he says.

I think I have seen something like this on *Grey's Anatomy*, but of course, I do not admit this. I am sure he hears things like that all the time.

I know myself.

I know I would panic.

I know I would freeze under that scalpel and puke in some kidney-shaped basin (in that lovely, familiar dull shade of pink) just as Dr. Bixton would yank out one of the weird tumor strings.

I will sleep, I tell him.

I will sleep as he studies me, as he pulls the monkey bread, the silly string, the cat hairball from my skull.

I desire to see nothing, to feel nothing, to wake up unhinged.

wake forest baptist hospital, neurology unit, the dash

JC is the last person I want to talk to before the surgeon extracts the tumor.

I have only known JC for three months, but here she is, with me in the hospital moments before the surgery.

This is weird, strange, bizarre.

Life is weird, she says as she sits by my bed. *Life is weird. I—life is weird.*

I met JC after my therapist prodded me to make an online dating profile after assuring me that *surely there are other single, academic people in their 30s in the Boone area.*

Sure, I thought. Sure.

I eventually swipe to JC's profile and do nothing.

I am confused, thrown.

Although I will later understand that JC is a *mood ring human*, whose looks seem to change whenever I see her, she looks a lot like me in her profile picture. She has a half-shaved head—the left side, just like mine—and lists the *Norton Critical Editions* as one of her interests. (Somehow this makes her look more like me, I guarantee.) She names Djuna Barnes' *Nightwood* as a favorite book and in a later private message, say *Oooh, Nightwood gets me every single time.*

I was convinced that myself and the six others in Dr. Moore's 2006 Modernist class in Marshall University's M.A. English program were the only ones to read *Nightwood*, but JC proves me wrong.

She teaches English somewhere in Boone and has a minty fresh Ph.D. in literature. I know she cannot teach in my department unless she skips every single Friday meeting and perhaps has an office in the basement of Sanford Hall instead of on the third or fourth floor. I try to figure out, to discover, where she might teach, but online searches yield nothing. High school? Community college? Surely no one moves to Boone for that, and JC definitely just moved to Boone.

I am not prepared to meet JC, so I avoid messaging her for weeks. This person seems too much like me, looks too much like me, might be me in some other dimension. Her profile finally appears for a third time when I am mindlessly swiping left, so I decide to send a *Hey, I also love Nightwood* message and wait for the albatross to hang around my neck and eventually drown me in uncertainty, waiting, fear.

A few weeks later, three of my cousins and I are sharing Thanksgiving dinner with JC, her friend Alex, and JC's family. We are not *a thing*— we made out once after a few beers but she *wasn't sure* what she *was emotionally ready for*, so I took the hint and became a friend.

Or something like that.

Now JC, who teaches the same classes I do but in the Harry Potter-ish residential college that lives its own existence on the far end of campus, sits on the edge of my cancer bed and listens to me worry about losing my language, my vocabulary, my writing skills.

Hopefully, it will just be your motor skills affected, even after surgery. I don't think you're going to lose your...language.

There has always been some element of the unsaid with JC. I do not understand, even after awkwardly kissing her and then driving home a little bit too drunk, my tiny car flying down the hill like a reckless baby bird, what exactly happened or didn't happen between us.

Sure, we can be friends.

Sure, we can be friends?

Sure. We can be friends.

Fremnds.

This is a word our dogs use to speak to one another on Instagram. It was just *frends*, but I added the *m*, the extra letter.

Two days after my birthday and the day before the seizure, JC and I go to my favorite restaurant in Boone. She was feeling *emotionally unavailable* and skipped my birthday party, so this is a mea culpa, a chance to settle things before the holidays.

I had a date the other night, and they spent the night, she says.

I figured.

I did not hear from JC for about a day, which was unusual, and I felt as if she was probably on a date and having a good time and forgetting about me completely because you know, dear tumor, we had much worse times to come but those lonely times *seemed really bad* and like we would never meet anyone or fall in love or feel close to anyone again.

We had each other, I suppose, but we did not know or understand this yet.

I woke up the next morning hating my ex, she says.

I alternate between drinks of beer and water. I use both of my hands. This is the last time I will use both hands for weeks. I will become a lefty for a short while and even practice making left-handed cursive letters prior to surgery.

JC remains attached to her ex; I know this, even understand this in a sick way. I am unnaturally attached to all of my exes and even people who weren't my exes, so I cannot fault JC for her inability to let go, to be free, to be alone and not quite ready to find someone new.

Before we leave the restaurant, I attempt to stand up from the table but falter. I assume this is because I have indulged in a couple beers to cleanse my feelings.

Of course, I assume wrong.

I am weak because I have a brain tumor I won't know about until the next morning.

As I hug JC goodbye, I step on her foot with my right snow boot but cannot move my foot away.

Life is weird, I think. *Life is weird. I—life is weird.*

About a week later, JC hugs me on my cancer bed for a long time. I hear the clock ticking—there are ticking clocks everywhere here— and I lose count of each heartbeat and second passing by.

I can't really tell if I am returning the hug or not; it's hard to understand, hard to know, hard to sense the stillness surrounding me.

I am afraid of everything and want to feel assured of something, anything.

JC cannot give me that.

She cannot give me anything but a stack of books to keep me busy through this extended hospital stay.

wake forest baptist hospital, pre-op, the dash

I tell at least twelve nurses *I am not pregnant.*

I lie on the surgery stretcher beside a guy getting his right leg amputated, or something like that. He moans and whines and cries and no one knows what to do with him.

I am about to let a surgeon crack into my skull and discover my secrets.

But are you pregnant?

They want to check my urine.

I insist *I am not pregnant*, which makes the medical staff ask me even more questions. My mom sits on one side, my friend and teammate Jenna on the other. My mom does not know my sexual history; Jenna knows everything.

I can't remember if they actually check my urine or not.

What I do remember: a very kind nurse anesthetist named Teddy, who put his palms under my head as I drifted off into blackness. How the surgery room resembled an amalgam of a high school gym and chemistry lab. The ceiling is much higher than I expect, the room larger and older than anything I have seen on television.

wake forest baptist hospital, post-op, the dash

I awake to an annoyed nurse who hates the way someone did my IV.

Do you respond to Susan? she asks me.

No, I most certainly do not.

I know you are feeling weird right now, but you need to respond to your name. Do you respond to Susan?

No, I do not. I never have.

Okay, you're not quite awake yet and someone really messed up this IV, sheesh, and you need to answer to Susan.

MY NAME IS NOT SUSAN GODDAMMIT.

Dr. Bixton removes most of you, tumor. He was smarter than you. He was better looking. He was more skilled.

You were his Grendel, his Jabberwocky, his reason to destroy. He wanted to save me, and he did—we just couldn't predict how long it would be before you tried to come back.

wake forest baptist hospital, ICU, the dash

I do not understand why it is so late.

I do not understand why my room in ICU looks like an office cubicle.

I do not understand why I keep grasping people's fingers, as if I am trying to transfer their liveliness to me.

I need them. I need you. I need a reason to survive this bullshit.

wake forest baptist hospital, ICU, the dash

My craniotomy takes forever, and I wake up wanting iced tea. I ask for it, beg for it, demand it.

No one will acquiesce.

How about you just give me water, and I'll pretend it's tea.

This feels like a high blood sugar: the dryness, the dehydration, the thirst.

It's from the intubation.

I guzzle the tea water someone finally gives me until the ICU nurse bitches at me for drinking too fast. I am sure she is worried I'm going to vomit up that tea water, maybe vomit up my feelings or some extra brain matter, but I just want to drink drink drink.

You, stupid motherfucking tumor, have made me thirsty, so thirsty for so much more.

I want to hold my friends' hands while I drink my tea water.

I still think my room in ICU looks like an office cubicle.

There is a poinsettia because it is three days before Christmas. There are mini blinds. There is a ticking clock that tells me it is after 11 p.m.

This surprises me—my surgery was supposed to take two hours and begin at 3 p.m. Surely, I have not lost this many hours, but I have. According to my mom, the surgery took such a long time *because Dr. Bixton wanted to make certain he got all of the tumor he could.*

And he did.

I have convinced myself I am done with this nonsense. I have convinced myself the tumor was benign. I convince myself I am finished with this mess.

It was not. I am not.

I am holding Feeney's hand and then Jenna's hand. I did not feel them switch. I have never been someone who needs an abundance of physical touch, but I want to feel their warm skin, the healthy pump of their heartbeat in their palm. I wish for that heartbeat to beat into me, to make me whole.

I want to be brave, but I also want to panic that there are staples in my scalp.

Fourteen.

Stop drinking so fast. You are going to vomit.

Fourteen staples holding my skin, my head, my brain together.

I can speak. I can think. I can do both of those things at the same time.

I want to hold my friends' hands and drink tea water.

I want to walk again.

I want to live.

wake forest baptist hospital, ICU, the dash

I have more feelings about you now that you are gone, tumor.

You splattered yourself into my frontal lobe, and I had no idea you existed.

Hello, hi, welcome to your brain, yes.

Here I am, you announced.

Aggressive, the surgeon said. *Powerful. Pervasive.*

You fucking asshole.

You looked like a cat hairball.

The surgeon and his team removed you fast, too quickly for us to become acquainted formally.

So let's talk, you and me. For just a moment. Our first date, our new encounter, our fresh start. We may move backward, sideways at some points. This process will be anything but linear, anything but straightforward.

We are both complicated; we have that in common.

Hi, I'm SZ. Most of my friends call me Hammer because I played roller derby for five years. My students at Appalachian State University, where I have taught English for six years, refer to me as Dr. SZ. I am (was? It's still too early to tell) blissfully teaching composition as a non-tenure track faculty member who enjoys having students stop by for paper conferences and chats about adjusting to freshmen life on campus.

I love cats (obviously, or I would not have made the earlier simile about hairballs), game shows, and this regional ginger ale energy drink called Dr. Enuf.

According to the Myers-Briggs Type Indicator, I am a classic INFJ.

I really like my eyelashes.

I have had type one diabetes for over thirty years.

I am a flash fiction writer, which suits my attention span and my inability to choose between fiction and poetry. (This also means chapters will be short, palatable, digestible.) Before I knew about you, I was on a publishing spree after a recent breakup. I was thriving; I was submitting and getting acceptances and even winning money.

I have been shaving the left side of my head for two years.

I like tempeh, but I am not a vegan or vegetarian.

The Hanged Man tends to show up in my tarot card readings, but I do not know what that means.

Most people might hate you, tumor; I am sure that I do, but you also interest me a great deal. Preliminary searches about you have told me that you prefer those over the age of fifty, so I am a bit surprised you chose me as your new friend. I am a bit surprised you somehow found me lurking in my tiny beautiful mountain town where people come to ski and escape the Florida hurricanes.

I am also a bit surprised you wanted to gift me with a leg seizure three days after my 36th birthday and send my life spiraling into a vast unknown of head staples, immobility, and quiet moments of malignant panic about thoughts, movement, survival.

Here I am, you announced.

You felt around my head, you searched for what I valued the most.

So nice to meet you, I said on December 18th, but I didn't trust you for a second. *I hope to never see you again*, I said on December 22nd, but there are never any guarantees, right?

wake forest baptist hospital, neurology unit, the dash

I touch my head and wonder what else might be inside.

This is weird, strange, unusual.

I remember before I learned about the tumor, before I knew, I would place my right index and middle finger where the tumor lived and press as if I was trying to turn on a coffee maker or a video game console. I thought I had minor sinus headaches, issues with mucous right above my eye. I would push that spot before falling asleep and remind myself to cleanse my nasal passages before school the next morning.

Gross.

When I tap that area after surgery, I feel nothing.

I will feel nothing so many times and so many ways in the days to come.

I am not angry I am not sad I am not awake.

wake forest baptist hospital, neurology unit, the dash

After surgery, I still cannot move my right hand.

I am right-handed, of course.

This is terrifying. I am a writer, a teacher. I type all day long. I need my hand to grade papers, to write flash fiction.

Sure, I thrived in my career as a teacher, but I always wanted to be a successful creative writer. To publish something of great measure, of panache. To have others read my work and feel a sense of purpose, a sense of connection. And now here I am flopped in a hospital bed, waiting for cold green beans to arrive for dinner.

A couple of my flash fiction publications were due to arrive in my mailbox the day of my brain surgery.

The stories waited in my mailbox with a bunch of hospital bills already eager to raid my bank account.

After my first post-surgery sleep, I awake with a hunger for writing and those cold green beans. I do not know my official diagnosis yet, but I know that writing this story is something I must do, have to do, am meant to do.

This is a story no one else can tell, no one else can design.

This is so fucked up.

I need to move my hand.

Slowly, the hand begins to twitch, to come back. I scratch my nose with my right hand and do not realize what I have done.

I heard you picked your nose! Jenna texts me.

I suppose my mom texted her. This is new to me: my mom being involved, my mom texting my friends.

I laugh.

I basically did pick my nose.

These are the moments I celebrate now.

Over the next few days, my hand is childish. I can barely move my fingers, manipulate my motions. I have no grip strength, but I slowly relearn how to hold a spoon and dig lime sherbet out of a Styrofoam cup. (I am not permitted to have lime sherbet per my diabetes hospital diet, but my mother sneaks it to me, my throat is still raw from the intubation. Later, my friends note that I seem to easily manipulate my mom, and they wonder if this is a pattern, a continuation of childhood. Not really, I tell them. Not really. She's just trying to make me happy, just trying to do what she can to help me feel a little bit like myself.)

The first time I try to sign my name, my once-elegant signature looks like the swirls and loops I made as a child on old waitressing pads that one of my dad's 8th-grade students gave him when she heard I had a kitchen set and wanted to *write orders*.

I once wrote in cursive.

I handwrote everything.

I've found that writing my flash fiction pieces by hand before typing them adds organic measure to my writing process. I'm not going to push that on anyone else or insist everyone should *handwrite their shit*, but I like the process of dumping my demons onto paper through the pen and then transferring out the junk, the extra adverbs and prepositions, once I move the writing from paper to the computer. This works efficiently for flash fiction—maybe not so much for longer works—and I once found great joy in staring at my gorgeous-yet-unreadable-to-others handwriting and knowing I was the only one who could decipher my codes, my symbols, my designs.

After surgery, I attempt to print.

When I try to write now, I turn my right hand so far to the left that my entire hand is almost backward. I do not tell my hand to do this—this is just how it happens. Although I am writing with my right, dominant hand, my print now resembles that of a left-handed child. Every letter, every word slants so far to the left that the letters, the words are almost vertically stacked atop one another.

And I am forming my letters backward.

Instead of making a capital "A" by starting at the bottom left and moving upward, I begin at the bottom right and draw backward. I can still form the letters correctly, but the process has flipped and become a mirror, a ghost of handwriting past.

As if I am in kindergarten again, I write my letters, both capital and lowercase, from Aa to Zz.

Backward, flipped, mirrored, slanted.

I practice.

I start again.

I am new.

wake forest baptist hospital, neurology unit, the dash
I love my catheter bag.

I never need to use the bathroom, but I do not think about this until two days after surgery.

Nothing hurts, not yet.

wake forest baptist hospital, neurology unit, the dash
Try to eat with your right hand, my mother instructs me.

I use my left hand to lift my fork.

No, your right hand.

This is my right hand.

No, that's your left.

I attempt to lift my right hand, but nothing happens.

This is my left hand, I insist.

I do not recognize anything but my mother's face, the first face I ever saw.

wake forest baptist hospital, neurology unit, the dash
The third time I fall in the neuro unit, no one is around to pull me up and tell me to get it together.

Once a nurse yanks out my catheter, I try to go to the bathroom on my own, and I know the staff has turned my beeping bed off.

They trust me.

They never should have trusted me.

I am a *two-assist*, which means I am so weak I require two nurses or nursing assistants to help me to the bathroom. But what if they are busy? What if they are admitting a new patient? What if they are doing paperwork or eating lunch or helping the 90-year-old vomiting man next door?

I try using the bathroom on my own, and I fail.

I can see where housekeeping has forgotten to scrub the small blue bathroom tiles. I am nowhere near a grab bar, and I do not know if I would be strong enough to lift myself up.

I hit the back of my head, and I fear that I may have smacked at least one staple.

Thankfully, there is no sign of blood, no sign of this disaster.

The first time I fell: my mother picked me up.

The second time I fell: my sister, who just arrived from Brooklyn, picked me up.

This third time: I finally wiggle my lame body to the emergency cord and admit *I fell in the bathroom* to the receptionist.

I have fallen so many times before.

In roller derby, everyone falls. Falling means trying, at first. And then falling means the skater is not bending their knees quite enough, not paying attention to the way their body reacts to the hits, to the action around them.

But the most important part of falling is learning to get up.

Even the best skaters fall; even the best skaters find themselves tossed to the floor during a practice or a bout; even the best skaters find those dirty spots on the ground to stare at for half a second before attempting to pull themselves up and rejoin the organized violence of the jam.

Falling is an important skill.

I fell twice at school on the same day, right before finals begin.

The first time, slightly more embarrassingly.

I am plodding up the stairs in my snow boots. Snow has not come for Boone yet, but it will. However, it is already cold, and I want to keep my feet warm; I want to be ready.

I am carrying books, papers, my laptop, things. I am walking up two flights of stairs at school, something I have done at least four times a day for six years.

And then I am on the ground. So are my laptop, books, papers, things.

SZ?

My colleague and friend Kate witnesses the accident. Students continue to stomp around me, the fallen professor, as Kate scurries to help me stand and pick up my belongings.

Kate makes me feel as if it is okay to have this sort of clumsy fall. She makes me feel as if I am allowed to make this type of mistake, even in front of students who just sat through my lecture about *using ethos, logos, and pathos in any real-world situation.*

Ethos: I've never fallen before, so it's just a freak accident. My reputation shows I am very reliable when it comes to not falling.

Logos: Logically, I have no reason to fall. There was a 99% chance I tripped over a dropped pen or piece of trash.

Pathos: Students should be helping me instead of staring at me. They should have empathy.

They don't.

Kate does.

She helps me to my office, where she places my books, my papers, my laptop, my things on my desk.

I feel a little dizzy, I say. *But I am okay.*

Kate, a poet who was a student of Charles Simic and is always a steadfast humanitarian, does not believe me. Her smile lies for her worried blue eyes.

These are the signs I did not notice.

Derby has prepared me for falling, I say. *I have gotten really good at falling.*

Thirty minutes later, Mel, another colleague and close friend, and I go to Stick Boy, the local coffee shop, to procure caffeine reinforcements for the afternoon. As I am holding my warm latte, I stumble off the lip of the sidewalk and onto the road. I hold onto the latte and keep my balance, but Mel notices.

Are you sure you are okay? he asks.

I am not sick I am not angry I am not dying.

I'm fine, just clumsy I guess.

After all, I caught myself the second time and recovered nicely.

Skating, I think. Skating.

Before the end of last season, my coach talked to me about falling. *I think you need to keep bending your knees while you are skating. You start off low, but then you pop up. Stay low, keep those knees soft.*

I was the type of skater who fell a lot.

Of course, I always got up.

Three weeks later I cannot walk at all.

Keep your knees soft, my first physical therapist in the neurology unit tells me. *Don't lock your knees.*

Stay low. Keep those knees soft.

The nurses and the doctors in the neurology unit are not happy with me after I tumble in the bathroom.

They shine a light into my eyes, ask me to follow, and tell me they hope I will not do this ever again.

wake forest baptist hospital, neurology unit, the dash

Christmas Eve: my sister sleeps on the hospital chair. The

tiny tree my friends brought blinks all night long to remind me the world moves, the world moves without me.

wake forest baptist hospital, neurology unit, the dash

I do not think about my brain on Christmas day.

I am certain the tumor is benign: my Christmas present to myself.

I sympathize with the nurses and doctors who slog through the hospital. I ask my nurses about their families and if they celebrated earlier. For them, this is just another day. Just another vitals check. Just another emptying of a catheter bag, the insertion of an IV.

My friend and teammate Mac brings me underwear.

Feeney brings cookies.

My friend Lori stops by on her way to see her brother.

Feeney brings chocolate.

My friend Ariel organizes my room and new underwear.

JC brings more books.

Carolers mill in the hospital hallway like fallen tree ornaments.

Hark! The herald angels sing!

I am festive or really high on medication: impossible to tell.

I got the tree up this year, my mom says, *but I did not get any decorations on the darned thing.*

Glory to the newborn king.

The old man next to me has no Christmas visitors, so my mom takes him a poinsettia.

Peace on earth and mercy mild.

God and sinners, reconciled.

I am certain the tumor was benign.

You'll find out after Christmas, a nurse tells us. *But it's probably good news if you haven't heard anything yet.*

I wish I could see a Christmas tree, a big, decorated one, but the little tree in my room and the wreath Feeney brought suffice. My medical staff loves my room. Sometimes, nurses come in just to see the decorations, just to feel as if they can take part in a holiday like anyone else, like the people outside of here who will never see the bruised nativity of my left arm.

wake forest baptist hospital, the dash

I move to the Sticht Center for Aging and Rehabilitation before New Year's. The girl who transports me notes that she *learned this hospital faster than anyone else in her program.*

How long did it take you? I ask her.

Three months, she replies without a smile or laugh.

steps

wake forest baptist hospital, sticht center, the dash

My first night in the rehabilitation center, Olaf drunk drives his wheelchair into my room.

This is what he tells me, anyway.

Drunk drivin and I crashed! I hear as he turns the wheelchair

and heads back to his room. 302. Right beside me.

Oh, Olaf.

Oh oh, Olaf.

I am guessing that when he leaves here, he will neither drink nor drive.

The night before the seizure, I had two beers with JC and then three PBRs with my teammates Mac and Dollfin when I got home. They wanted to come over and bitch, to come over and see my new kitten that I gave back to her foster mom once the initial diagnosis became a reality.

Mac, Dollfin, and I sat around that night and used our phones to play old, white sad bastard songs from the 90s. I think we listened to Counting Crows' "Long December" at least five times. Someone Snapchatted it, and I accidentally sent it to my latest ex because I had no idea what I was doing.

We are going to be single and lonely forever.

Why do people hate us?

Life could not get worse than this.

Before everything *went to shit*, I would occasionally indulge in nights like these. After all, I was 36, divorced, lonely, heartbroken, and only into the underdeveloped ideas of people.

Things felt pretty bad.

Mac and Dollfin are 14 years younger than I am but know the old sad white bastard 90s music because it somehow became cool again. They can work Snapchat and gripe at me for accidentally sending the Snapchat of Mac's Adam Duritz impression to my stupid ex.

JC later tells me that she finished off the final three PBRs while I was in the hospital. She came over to clean and there was the beer. Good, I think. Good. I'm glad it was JC. I'm glad it was someone who cares.

Olaf does not drunk drive again after my first night, but he does wheel his chair into my room some nights, just to see what I am up to.

wake forest baptist hospital, the sticht center, the dash

I wake up at the rehabilitation center furious with Chole.

Pronounced *Cole*, of course.

I said goodbye to you, brain tumor, six days ago.

Did you cause me problems with Chole, tumor? We do not know when you began to grow, when you made yourself a shelter in my brain. It would be convenient to blame my adoration of Chole on you, but I do not know if you deserve that.

Chole blamed me for everything, of course.

That's what narcissistic sociopaths do.

She accused me of *being a drama queen and just needing to accept that about myself.* Chole cursed me for *victimizing myself for no reason, we weren't even together that long, dammit.* Chole impugned me for *refusing to let her go, stalking her, and breaking into her house to see the kittens.*

I did not do any of those things.

Well, fine. I did a couple of those things, but I did not stalk her or break into her house. I was playing in my final derby bout the day she accused me of breaking in and being a psycho. Not even a tumor could make me that crazy.

I refused to let her go. I was a little bit of a drama queen, but I think anyone would be if they had to drag their blacked-out drunk partner home and then put her to bed while she was screaming at you and calling you *a fucking piece of shit* because she was too drunk to be dishonest.

I think anyone would be a drama queen if they then opened up their partner's phone and saw she had been soberly Sunday-morning texting her ex-girlfriend about missing the feeling of *fingering her in the employee bathroom* of her last service industry job and never forgetting about *how good they were at being in love.*

Sure, asshole, I'll put your pajama pants on you while you scream at me for being a *fucking piece of shit* and think about your ex-girlfriend's vagina. Sure. I'll even refuse to let you go for weeks after I set you a morning alarm and left your wasted, bloated body in the center of the bed because that's where you seem comfortable, and the incessant, drunk snoring is *what I signed up for dammit, because people have problems and I can deal with that shit.*

I do not know if you, tumor, and Chole existed simultaneously.

All I know is Chole conveniently dumped me—or actually, allowed me to dump myself so she did not have to deal with the messiness of my feelings—three months before I found out about you.

I tell one of my friends I'm worried I will never have sex again. She laughs at me. *I did not think that was something you would worry about,* she says. *Especially now.*

But it's everything I am worried about.

I want the feeling of weightlessness, of losing myself. I want the feeling of trusting someone with my body, my desires. I want the feeling of forgetting.

Chole was the worst, and she cannot be my last.

A friend told Chole what happened. Chole apparently turned as white as my marker board in the hospital room.

Another friend told Chole, and she acted surprised.

But you can only be surprised about this type of thing once.

Still, I expected Chole to take a shot and say with an eye-roll that she didn't *give a fuck.*

Let's be clear, though—Chole does not give a fuck. According to social media, she started dating her friend Sienna a couple months after allowing me the honor of dumping myself. Although Chole cried whenever I tried to have sex with her and claimed to be *so vanilla, dude,* now Chole posts pictures of ball gags and anything else of sexual shock value to her paltry amount of Instagram followers.

I'm sorry for what you're going through, I hope you heal fast, she messages me after unblocking me from all forms of social media.

I fucking hate myself for dating someone who has no idea how to avoid the dangers of a comma splice.

Later, she posts a picture collage of her best nine Instagram photos from 2017.

2017 was a dumpster fire, she writes, *but it was my dumpster fire.*

Although I spent half of 2017 engulfed in that dumpster fire, I am in none of the pictures.

wake forest baptist hospital, the sticht center, the dash
DO YOU KNOW WHERE YOU ARE?

The physical therapy doctor asks every morning.

Everyone, every morning.

HUH? Olaf asks.

Wake Forest Baptist Hospital.

DO YOU KNOW WHAT YEAR IT IS?

2017 but almost 2018.

WHO IS THE PRESIDENT?

GEORGE W. BUSH, someone answers.

I refuse to say the president's name.

Should have been Hillary or Bernie, I say.

The doctor does not yell at me the next day.

wake forest baptist hospital, the sticht center, the dash
What are you going to blame being a bitch on now that they took the tumor out?

Although I am unsure of the time, it's the middle of the night, which means one thing—Chole is plastered like one of my college freshmen. Except Chole is not young and Chole is not naïve—Chole is in her 30s and uses alcohol to erase feelings about drug addiction, ex-girlfriends, time spent in prison for heroin, feelings about her parents' divorce, anything, everything, all the things.

Chole has never known a life of pure uncertainty.

Yet she has made poor choices and even poorer excuses. A trust fund keeps her travel plans and pill problem floating in that ocean of bad decisions. Sure, the trust fund does not pay for Xanax or vodka pineapples, but it pays the electric bill. The dog's vet bills. The things that typically worry those caught between Generation X and the Millennials.

Almost all of us.

Not Chole. She does not and did not need to worry about these problems.

Why not them why not them why not them.

The only thing I did: I sent Chole *too many* emails.

I think I sent nine, all in response to things she said, to actions she performed.

And then the accusation: I broke into her house. She makes this jab because she found a diabetes testing strip in her bedroom. I knew the exact strip she described. I had forgotten to pick it up months before we broke up and told myself I would deal with the diabetes detritus later. Test strips, as any type one diabetic knows, are the constant litter of diabetes. I once found a test strip in my shoe from a glucose machine I had not used for at least twenty years.

Chole accused me of harassing her, stalking her.

I would not have wasted my time.

You know that sending me too many emails is harassment, right?

You know that falsely accusing someone of breaking into your house is slander, right?

I don't hear from Chole after that.

Until you showed up, brain tumor, and wrecked everything, you fucking bitch.

I suppose you're lucky you didn't get saddled with a brain cancer girlfriend, I write to Chole. *I'm only being sarcastic with you, just like old times. But you did get lucky. You would have hated me even harder, I suppose.*

But it was never clear, before you came along, dear tumor, why Chole hated me, except that her ex-girlfriend broke up with her own rebound and suddenly reappeared in Chole's phone to talk about how she *missed being fingered in the Tastee Diner bathroom* and how *good they were at being in love.*

I wondered why I had not heard from Chole that morning, but I assumed it was because she knew I was at derby practice and did not want to bother me. After all, the previous night, Chole had messaged me to say that she would build me a library one day and we *would get married* because she also wanted a library and we were *so much alike in these ways* that *we were meant to be together.*

We had planned to move in together in January 2018.

I was going back to Asheville; Chole wanted to kick out her beloved 22-year-old roommate and have me take her place. I would commute to Boone for work, and we would cook each other things and be in love and take care of one another. Chole wanted to try derby, and I would support her and help her learn how to plow stop and halt an opposing jammer from getting through the pack.

Chole was an actor, a better actor than I originally thought.

Chole is still a sociopath, still a narcissist who stares at her own Instagram pictures to *see just how green and gorgeous* her eyes are in each post.

Now her new girlfriend does drag, and Chole makes social media posts about *oh my god drag is so amazing!!!!!! i love it!!!!*, and I finally realize Chole is nothing more than a sad little chameleon, the type of creature who just morphs into whatever their significant other enjoys and loves.

After all, drinking vodka pineapples, hitting the bong, and popping Xanax do not constitute hobbies.

I do not remember how I respond to Chole after she writes *What are you going to blame being a bitch on now that they took the tumor out?*, but she went too far. Way too far. My prior message was a bit sarcastic, but that is how we always communicated with one another. I found familiarity in that sarcasm; however, Chole's message arrives too late at night and without a precursor.

I take her seriously, especially because she blocks me on Instagram directly after sending the message.

She does not mention that she also relies on sarcasm or is just testing my boundaries.

No.

She just wants to be a cunt.

She is a terrible person.

She is the worst.

Immediately after blocking me on Instagram, Chole posts a meme to Facebook.

To further convince any reader of Chole's awfulness, the meme uses Comic Sans font.

Don't victimize yourself due to circumstances you created.

Chole adds a couple fun emojis to assure everyone she is in charge, she is in control.

I cannot help myself.

This craniotomy made me not really give a shit about who knows all of Chole's faults, her problems, her sick addictions.

And then I got a brain tumor?

Yeah, I totally created those circumstances.

Let me tell you, having a brain tumor and knowing you may not have much time left makes you not give a shit about being honest with people and YOU are the fucking piece of shit. You victimize yourself by being an addict and inhaling any substance that comes your way. You lie about everything and just tell people what they want to hear in any given moment.

You should feel incredibly lucky for the life you have, but you waste every single second of it.

Nice knowing you.

I do have the thought that Chole should have gotten brain cancer. Not me. Someone terrible.

I was never perfect in relationships, but I was nice to Chole. Caring. Polite.

When she caused me to break up with myself after calling me a *worthless piece of shit*, I disappeared. I only returned to give back stuff, which she insisted I was trying to steal; I did not bother her except for those *too many emails*—that were actually more explanatory of my feelings, of me *still being in love* after being unceremoniously dumped—and did not bother her otherwise, no matter how much she insisted I did.

But Chole always needs to feel important, and a part of me wonders if she regretted not being with me during the brain surgery shit because it was something very, very important, and she was not, definitely not, any part of the process.

I receive a deluge of private messages from Chole's friends after I publicly blast her.

you're supposed to be a grownup!!!

SZ your acting like a child!!!

take it down, now!

you should never publicly shame someone like that!

I do not say this, but I wonder the difference. I wonder the difference between my meme reply and Chole publicly humiliating herself every single night at the bar, her full 170 pounds flopped beneath a barstool like a dying baby elephant. (Her signature gray hoodie only adds to this visual.) I wonder the difference between my meme reply and Chole screaming at her friends on the porch about how her green eyes are *far more beautiful than anything you fuckers have to offer*. I wonder the differences between my meme reply and Chole smoking crack with her neighbor in the middle of her street, both of them blinking so fast I thought they were having seizures.

I do not say this, but I wonder the difference.

wake forest baptist university, the sticht center, the dash

My marker board today:

Surgeon: Bixton

Secretary: Margie

Our goals:

Today: ? Rehab

Your Stay: SAFETY

I stare at this board for minutes, hours, days.

wake forest baptist hospital, sticht center, the dash

Late at night as I hear the life flight helicopter land a few feet away from my rehabilitation room, I scroll through Tinder. I have a surprising number of matches in The Dash, but I feel guilty when the matches message me.

What are you up to tonight?

Oh, just chilling in an adjustable hospital bed. The bed might explode when I stand, so no, I cannot meet you tonight.

I like your cat.

Thank you, I have not seen her in two weeks. I'm sure she hates me now.

Want to grab a beer?

Let me ask Linda, my CNA, if I can get a bar pass for the night.

I don't respond to any of them. I wish I could; I wish I could stroll out of this lockdown and drink a craft beer at the corner bar. I wish I could even have a phone conversation without someone at the nurse's station listening to me chat about *attempting to walk 13 feet today* or discovering that I am *locked in a fancy nursing home and trying to learn to use my hand again.*

I do not respond to any Tinder messages, but I edit my profile:

What do I have in common with Jeopardy's Trebek? We both just had brain surgery!

I still think I'm pretty fun, though.

wake forest baptist hospital, sticht center, the dash

I dream of Alex, JC's friend who spent Thanksgiving with us.

Everything is going to be okay, Alex tells me.

This is the first time I have believed anyone.

wake forest baptist hospital, sticht center, the dash

Somehow, I end up with Bentley.

We are an odd pair.

He's a couple years younger than I am and as gruff as my dead grandfather.

But Bentley has these moments during our physical therapy sessions where I see the pink, fluffy ventricles of his heart hiding behind his hairy skin and blank brown eyes. I learn about his wife, his son, and his daughter as I struggle to ride the stationary bicycle, take a single step without the walker or the wheelchair, and do glute bridges on a therapy table.

Bentley cares.

He also has a sense of humor and laughs at some of my jokes.

He talks about his sassy daughter and how she is just like his wife.

Bentley watches me do those glute bridges *one two three four* and notes in my chart that I *am progressing*.

He inspires me, though I am not sure why.

He tests my balance and strength.

You received a two out of ten the first time you took this test a week ago, he says.

Thank god he did not tell me then. Always motivated by external achievement and progress, a 2/10 would have broken me.

I close my eyes and attempt to balance as long as I can.

Bentley catches me before I fall over. I could have done this task for twenty minutes before the tumor, before the craniotomy.

Now I can barely stand there for three seconds without losing my balance.

It's okay, he says. *You still got a ten out of twelve today. That's much better.*

Bentley lets me walk in the afternoons. We stroll around the Sticht Center as he tracks the number of feet I walk with the walker, with the leg braces, and sometimes, without anything at all.

One-hundred and fifty feet today, he says.

It sounds like nothing, *one-hundred and fifty feet*, but the week before, I could not get out of bed without two nurses assisting me. I could not walk a single step; I struggled to get from my bed to a chair merely three inches away.

I give Bentley a high-five, and I can tell he is proud of the work I have done today.

wake forest baptist hospital, sticht center, the dash

My first Asian nurse tells me I remind her *of someone back home.*

My second Asian nurse tells me my smile reminds her of her *best friend* during her teenage years. I smile again. *You look just like her*, she says as she grabs my hand.

To my knowledge, I have no Asian ancestry, but I do purchase a DNA kit when I return home so I can discover the truth of myself, the lineage of my personal history.

We all feel compelled to know these trees, these branches, these roots at some point.

Both nurses make this connection with such confidence, with such gravitas, that I convince myself I must have some connection to Asian culture.

Somehow.

Somewhere.

Someplace.

Or maybe I am just dying and my soul is being dragged back to where I belong, somewhere I have never been, somewhere I need to return to as I lose my sense of self, my sense of existence, my sense of who the fuck I am.

You remind me of someone.

Most days, I do not even know who I am or what I am doing. This was consistent before surgery, before the brain tumor, before the surgeon cut me open and plucked out that nasty hairball tumor.

It's your smile.

It's always my smile.

You just look so much like her.

I don't mind this at all. I convince myself that if I remind each nurse of *someone back home*, of a *best friend*, then they will give me what I need. They will bring my insulin to me faster, they will be gentler with the blood sugar checks, and they will not mind so much when I need assistance to take a piss.

And maybe they will comfort me.

Nights in the hospital, even with the buzzes and thumps of the life flight helicopter, even with the irritating tick of the elementary school clock, even with the nurses coming in every hour to check my blood pressure, blood sugar, or temperature, get loudly lonely.

You remind me.

Maybe they tell all patients this. Maybe this is like the *let's check your blood sugar and see how sweet you are today!* joke the nurses tell to make the patient feel more at ease.

But I feel a presence, a connection with these nurses who claim I remind them of someone.

Your smile.

I am certain they just want to make me feel more comfortable, more at ease.

My sister left the day after Christmas. She washed my hair, although the nurses told her no, and she was careful to avoid wetting my fourteen head staples.

My mom visits the rehab center during the day and stays as long as she can at night, but I am still afraid.

The nurses must know this.

I'm sure there is a note in my file.

You remind me of someone back home.

My best friend.

We are here to see how sweet you are today.

I am here for some reason: perhaps to remove a brain tumor, perhaps to learn how to walk again, perhaps to find myself and discover what I was meant to become, what I was meant to discover, what I was meant to see.

You look just like her.

wake forest baptist hospital, sticht center, the dash

My occupational therapist, Angel, thinks I am a free spirit.

No one has ever called me this before.

Angel is around my age, and I say whatever I want to her. For some reason, I feel comfortable enough to joke and listen to music on my iPod while we work.

Why I am comfortable with Angel: she gives me showers.

With Angel's help, I am allowed to wash my hair.

In other words, Angel is allowed to wash my hair, as long as the staples remain dry.

I bond with her immediately.

I spend afternoons with Angel in the rehab center's model grocery store. She watches me use a grab stick to pull down empty boxes of rice to check the price and see if I can afford this meal from my fake checking account that has $53.23.

Today I can.

What I can't do: find the Garnier conditioner that's on my shopping list.

Although I have been practicing walking, I am not allowed to leave the wheelchair without professional assistance. At the fake grocery store,

I wheel myself around and sift through the hair products. I even check the food aisles to see if someone has misplaced the conditioner.

I know I just had brain surgery and all, but I don't think this Garnier conditioner actually exists.

Angel stops what she is doing to help me search for the lost green conditioner.

You know what? You're right, she says.

I thought maybe it was a trick to see just how well my brain surgery worked, I say.

Angel laughs.

She teaches me to put on my shoes. She helps me get dressed in the morning. She lets me avoid doing the woodworking task in the occupational therapy room because she knows I hate that kind of shit.

Angel allows me to stand from the chair and sweep my room so I can feel useful.

On a Thursday, Angel helps me do a pretend load of laundry. We find a pair of dirty men's underwear in a pile of clothes that is supposed to be clean and available for patients in need.

Oh my god, Angel says as I pick up the underwear with the grab stick. *Oh my god.*

She opens the garbage bin so I can drop the underwear into the trash.

We make a good team.

You know someone is going to ask about that later, I say. *For the first time ever, someone is going to say* HEY HAVE YOU SEEN THAT DIRTY PAIR OF MAROON MEN'S UNDERWEAR? A PATIENT WAS LOOKING FOR THOSE.

Angel and I both laugh away the long afternoon.

wake forest baptist hospital, sticht center, the dash
I am sweating I am trying to take a shit I am dying.

Or at least that's how I feel.

Do you want your blood sugar checked? Alicia, my nursing assistant for the day, asks. Alicia also has type one diabetes. *I think you're having a low.*

I am on the toilet I am sweating I am in pain.

I do not think there is any possible way I am having a low blood sugar. This should be the least of my worries, though it is not. The endocrinology team at the hospital has refused to let me wear my insulin pump—a machine resembling a first-generation iPod that delivers a constant feed of insulin through a self-inserted steel needle that I change every three days—because that's *just not what we do here.*

They have not consulted my doctor: an endocrinologist who happens to be in the same town, but works for the competing medical system.

I bitch I complain I whine.

Occasionally, I have fussed about my regular endocrinologist to friends, family, my Starbucks barista. But at the end of the day when my blood sugar is 341 and I'm staring at that stupid gondola painting on the rehab center wall and I'm wondering why I'm still on a goddamned steroid, I want to see my endocrinologist more than anyone else. He knows me—he knows that I hate checking my blood sugar in the morning, knows I hate inputting my glucose values into my pump, knows I take issue with nurses pricking the soft pads of my fingers instead of the sides. My doctor is young, he's hip, and he probably graduated medical school when I was celebrating my 25th anniversary with diabetes, but whatever.

After a year under his care (and one appointment where I sobbed the entire twenty minutes and begged him to *let me try something different*), I decide I like him.

And want him here.

But no one else agrees with me.

I am on the toilet, and I am convinced I am not having a low.

I try to push out shit but nothing happens.

I sit on the toilet and squeeze as hard as I can, but only tears come out. Nothing else.

This is what happens in the hospital. I lose all sense of decency, decorum. Everyone who works on this floor has seen me piss down my leg, has seen me attempt to insert a tampon with my left hand, has seen puke running down my arm after a long day of physical therapy.

They have seen it all.

Of course, I know they have seen worse. Still, I remark that this is something new, something embarrassing for me. They know this, they understand this, they seem to expect that every patient will give a monologue regarding piss, shit, and blood at some point.

My blood sugar is a dangerously low 33. The nursing assistant checks while I attempt to shit.

I drink orange juice on the toilet, and I know that nothing could ever be more embarrassing than this.

Trying to take a shit while drinking juice on the toilet while trying to convince the nursing assistant that my blood sugar is not low.

I am not a liar; low blood sugar turns one into a demonic asshole.

The nursing assistant uses a baby wipe to clean me up while I keep drinking my juice. She tosses me into my wheelchair and transports me back to bed.

My main nurse comes in with graham crackers and peanut butter. She quickly spreads the peanut butter over the graham crackers as if she is preparing a snack for a petulant child after school.

Why is no one helping me? I scream. *Why is no one helping me?* Everyone in the room is helping me; everyone is trying to do their best.

I have seen this on crime shows, I say as bits of graham cracker tumble from my mouth to my clean, white sheets. *Insulin is untraceable. These nurses want to get on crime shows, so they give me too much insulin, and then this happens. Then I look like a fool.*

Everyone in here is helping you, my mom says. She has seen this type of behavior before.

I do not believe her.

I am going to vomit, I announce. I am going to vomit.

My mom grabs a pink basin from the bathroom. As she holds the basin under my chin, I puke up the soup I had for lunch.

The vomit trails down my chin and into the curves between my breasts, through and underneath my hospital gown. I cannot help this; I cannot do anything to stop this from happening. My nurse forces a peanut butter graham cracker into my mouth. I chew compliantly. I have no other choice.

My mom scrubs my face with another baby wipe; I do not tell her about the puke that has trailed to where I once wore a bra.

I really don't see the point.

We could reinsert your IV and give you glucose through the line, my nurse says.

Even with a blood sugar of 33, I have no interest in this. I would rather puke all over myself again, or even shit the bed before having another IV inserted.

I had four IVs when I first arrived at the rehabilitation center, and I convinced a different nurse each time to take one out until I had zero. So far, this has been my greatest achievement since being admitted as a patient.

We will check again in twenty, my nurse says.

I am sure she hates me; I would.

Why, why is no one helping me?

Everyone is doing their best, my mom says. *You just have to trust them. Relax.*

JC was supposed to visit today with her dog. I was disappointed when she told me she didn't think they could make it. I sat in the bottom floor of the Sticht Center in my wheelchair and waited for nothing. It was the year anniversary of when she gave her wife an ultimatum, and her wife, well, she did not comply. JC didn't think she could get out of bed today, and she was very sorry, but maybe she could come another time? She was very sad. And sure, I just had brain surgery, but who cares about that?

Who cares about brain surgery when your wife leaves you after you give her an ultimatum? Who cares about something so silly?

Another time, of course.

It is best this way, I convince myself. I do not want anyone to see me with vomit and orange juice smeared all over my face and neck.

It is best I be alone today.

wake forest baptist hospital, sticht center, the dash

There was a man here to see you, my nurse says. *He was carrying a briefcase. He said he did not want to interrupt your speech therapy. I've never seen him before.*

It must have been my friend and neurologist Jon, I think. Just stopping by to see what I was up to, see how I was doing.

wake forest baptist hospital, sticht center, the dash

I smile when I see Dr. Bixton walk through the door of the rehabilitation center. He has come to tell me how my brain tumor was benign, and now I can get back to my life and learning to walk again.

The Man with the Briefcase.

I expected to wait longer for this good news; I did not anticipate a late Christmas present, a happy way to start the new year.

If you just think positive, so many people told me, *you will get better. It won't be cancer.*

My gut, my soul, my life blueprint told me *don't worry. You are okay. Everything was benign.*

I believed everyone; I believed myself.

I removed all of the tumor I could, Dr. Bixton tells me. *Unfortunately, the tumor is what's known as a grade IV glioblastoma. It was malignant. You have brain cancer and will require chemotherapy and radiation. Try your best to avoid Googling grade IV glioblastoma. Typically, patients live for about a year after diagnosis, if they take chemo and radiation to slow tumor regrowth.*

I cannot stop shaking I cannot stop shaking I cannot stop shaking.

The Man with the Briefcase.

The shaking increases the shaking increases the shaking in creases.

Happy New Year.

I'll stop here, Dr. Bixton says. *We can talk about treatments when you are ready.*

I'll never be ready I'll never be ready I'll never be ready.

My nurse that night gives me a valium and asks *how is your faith?*

I lost faith in myself that afternoon.

wake forest baptist hospital, the dash

Before she leaves, my mom nearly wheels me into my surgeon in the hallway of the ubiquitous hospital maze.

Wake Forest Baptist, as I learn, has its own zip code. It is a city of sick people, a metropolis of professionals, surgeons, nurses, and transporters. The hospital is a town full of families and hopeful patients who want, more than anything, to improve their quality of life. Like me, they might live here for a while—long enough, at least, to give the new zip code to friends and loved ones who want to send their best.

I convince my mom to take me to the Starbucks kiosk about every other day. We could go each day, but I don't always feel strong enough to climb from the bed to the wheelchair after hours of physical, occupational, and speech therapy.

My mother pushes the wheelchair so fast that it seems she believes the following: if she pushes quickly enough, if she is strong enough, she can push me away from these diseases, from these blood sugar problems, from this cancer that will likely kill me.

Or perhaps her gait as a former competitive race walker takes over, and she cannot help herself.

A combination of both.

Today I do not attempt to be careful. I do not know what my stomach can tolerate, but FUCK IT, I just found out I have brain cancer, and I want a goddamned frappucino. I worked at Starbucks for a year and never drank frappucinos; I preferred the iced teas and cold brew coffees, like a proper 90s hipster who still listens to Elliott Smith and Conor Oberst.

But now, more than anything, I want a fucking frappucino.

I order a decaf espresso one with soy milk.

This is as careful as I can be right now.

I puke up the entire drink four hours later, but I enjoy the cool rebellion as the blended mix slides down my still-raw throat.

When we run into Dr. Bixton, though, I am happy, relaxed, and a little jolted from the infinitesimal amount of caffeine that still exists in decaf.

I am ready to listen.

When the Man with the Briefcase first visited my room in the rehabilitation center, I was not ready to listen. Not prepared to listen. Not accepting of the given diagnosis.

Today I am ready.

We sit across from the owls in the tunnel. My mom uses the owl portraits as a landmark to ensure she is headed the correct direction in the hospital. I swear the owls watch her wheel me around and feel their own sense of motion sickness.

You will have roughly 33 radiation treatments and chemo for six months.

Even recalling this, I am not certain of my facts. I remember the 33, I remember the six months. Did I have the chemo and radiation switched? Surely not.

You'll work with Dr. Crowder for the radiation and Dr. Stroupe for the chemo.

Doctors, doctors, doctors

Now I did get most of the tumor removed during surgery—all I could find. This will help.

This will help.

Dr. Bixton is careful to avoid saying *this will prolong your survival.* Doctors say phrases like that in the movies, but not in hospital hallways with their own zip codes and owl portraitures.

We are going to do all we can to help you. You'll start chemo and radiation at the end of January. Remember that the diagnosis, the chemo, and the radiation should not hinder your process of walking again or beginning to feel better after surgery.

Dr. Bixton is nice.

He is really, really nice.

But I realize the discussion of treatments *should not hinder your process of walking again or beginning to feel better after surgery* is a clever way to distract me from the process of dying.

I understand why he does this; I tell my students *whatever grade I give on your first paper should not hinder your process of working hard and doing well on the second paper.*

We are all just hoping to survive, hoping to make it out and find the little bit of light promised to us by some authority figure, by someone who knows just a little bit more than we do, someone we hope we can trust with our survival.

wake forest baptist hospital, sticht center, the dash

Keke wants to know why I am here.

There are certain similarities between the rehab facility and prison. Of course, no one deserves a stay here, and the nurses spend their grueling twelve-hour shifts ensuring we remain comfortable and alert and safe.

However, we cannot leave.

Patient prisoners remain tethered to IV tubes, locked into wheelchairs, glued to walkers, or confined to beeping white beds.

Of course, most of us are physically unable to reach the door of our room without an hour's effort. If we tried, blaring alerts would fracture the nurses' chatter about their leftovers and *Papaw in 305*; a buzzer would sound like a fire alarm; or, someone at the desk would see us wobbling out like drunken teenagers trying to leave a boring house party.

They would belt us back before the next meal, med round, or doctor's visit.

The staff locks the main door, and one can only escape by calling the front desk from a well-placed phone—out of reach for anyone in a wheelchair, which most of us are—or through swiping a key card.

Thirty feet from the nurses' station, the main door and elevators sit like Bruce Springsteen's promised land, a goal we can dream about yet never achieve. If they played music here, which they don't, Roy Orbison would background visions of white dresses, Chevrolets, and dirt roads we imagine but never see.

This distance remains too far for any of us to attempt an escape. If we decide, for example, to exit our rubber beds in the middle of the night to take a piss, alarms sound and at least two nurses sprint to the room. At all hours of the night, I hear their shoes squeak like lonely words and burned-out car engines as they try to prevent their charges from falling onto the scuffed floors.

FALL RISK bracelets are issued, and one feels like a fool for trying to do something as simple as walk to the bathroom and yank down pajama pants.

The biggest unspoken rule, though, is part penal institute, part *Fight Club*: no one—patients, nurses, or doctors—ask others why they are here.

Keke cannot help herself.

Most of the staff knows *why* through copious notes in each of our files, but not one person employed at the rehabilitation center utters the words *tumor, cancer,* or *craniotomy.*

The only professional to speak in this lexicon is Dr. Bixton, my surgeon who tells me and my mother in the privacy of 301—my bedroom, my studio apartment, my American dream—that although he *got all the tumor*, it is a *grade four glioblastoma, a very aggressive type of brain cancer*, and I will require *chemo and radiation* but might qualify for *clinical trials*. He mentions that the *median survival rate* for glioblastomas is 12 to 15 months, but he does assure me that my young *age will help*. He also warns me to *stay off the internet*, although he knows that as soon as he leaves, that is exactly where I will go.

There was a guy here to see you, the nurse says. *He was carrying a briefcase.*

The Canadian Man with the Briefcase.

Dr. Bixton is not American enough for two-lane roads and their magic one only finds at night.

Keke understands this.

*

I have confused Keke.

She works as a tech for the physical therapists—that's my guess, anyway. She contorts walking devices, pops and locks canes, sanitizes walkers, maneuvers prosthetics, and transports patients in wheelchairs all day.

She does not have access to my file.

Most of the convalescents here are elderly men. Sadly, there are occasionally children or teenagers, but mostly, the literature decorating the common tables and the wheelchairs at breakfast indicate the following: men over the age of 60 dominate the population. They once offered redemption from underneath dirty car hoods, now they slump in wheelchairs and only see rain from the tinted windows that have not been cleaned since last Wednesday.

I have kept track.

Do you mind if I ask you what happened? Keke whispers after escorting me back to my room and making certain I am safely back in my alert-heavy bed.

I do not mind her asking.

Keke is not my friend; I do not know her, and we have rarely spoken.

But outside of here, we would like one another. In high school, we would have talked about cute football players and smoked Newports in the girls' bathroom after government class. Keke played softball in college, just began a workout boot camp, and has a thunderous smile. If I met her at that boot camp, we would have cried into a margarita after deep lunges and lazy leg lifts.

I don't mind at all, I say. *I woke up one day, was having coffee with a friend, then had a leg seizure. Twenty minutes later, I'm in the emergency room, and some random doctor is telling me there is a mass in my brain. No headaches, no blurry vision, nothing but some weakness in my right leg about a week before. I ended up here at Baptist and had a craniotomy a few days later. The surgeon removed the tumor, but it was cancerous. I'm going to start chemo and radiation soon. I couldn't move my right side at all after the seizure, but my right arm came back about three days after surgery. My leg, of course, is still...not listening.*

This is the short story, of course.

Keke's mouth hangs open, and the spaces intruding her beautiful teeth remind me of the gaps between the locks on my walker.

You had no symptoms, she says. She does not ask this as a question; instead, she frames this as a statement, but one that I still need to answer.

Nope, not really. Just some weakness in my leg. I've been a type one diabetic for 31 years, so I thought it was—

—neuropathy, she finishes.

I know, I just know, that Keke and I would be friends outside of this sterile anodyne prison.

You should go get a CT scan, an MRI, all the things, I say. *I know insurance doesn't cover them, but just in case.*

The next day, my physical therapist puts Keke in front of me and tells me to push on her hands as I attempt to walk. I imagine myself in fitness boot camp with her and shove my weight into her being as if we are the same person with the same struggles with the same desire to ask what no one else dares.

A full week later, I am walking unassisted except for an air cast and a brace that pulls my toes away from the ground in a weird defiance of gravity and hope.

You showin out, girl, Keke proudly says. *You showin out.*

It's late, I think. I imagine us taking the long walk to her car and skipping the fitness boot camp to yell the names of our past lovers into empty, wet streets.

We can make it if we run, I think. We can make it if we run.

wake forest baptist hospital, sticht center, the dash

Speech therapist: Name something salty.

Me: White girls.

wake forest baptist university, sticht center, the dash

My sister Sarah, the Brooklyn hairstylist, snorts cocaine with a cute Mexican to cope with her complicated feelings.

I don't feel sick I don't feel sick I don't feel sick.

This is all I can think for the near month I am here in the hospital and rehabilitation center.

Besides my possessed right leg, besides the 31 years of type one diabetes, I am normal. Achingly average at most things. Go to work, go to derby practice or the gym, go home. Spend time with my cats. Read books. Indulge my fun nerdy side with mystery solving deductive reasoning subscription boxes where I have to solve a fake crime with tactile clues. Browse Tinder and OKCupid in hopes that someone might pay attention to me. Drink nitro cold brews from Starbucks. Listen to a lot of Sufjan Stevens.

Average, but indie average.

My sister is angry.

I have not felt angry I have not felt angry I have not felt angry.

How did you sit in my brain, tumor? How long were we together? How long did you know me? How long? How long? How long?

Were you there when I visited Sarah in New York City and slapped her across her pale face when she got too drunk and pissed me off? Can I blame you for that? Were you there when I sent Chole *too many emails* after she made me break up with myself, and when she cowardly let me discover the truth about who she was? Were you there when I got irritated with one of my students for not knowing what a record was and insisting that Lynyrd Skynyrd was *a really cool band from the 90s*?

Or would anyone without you taking up space in their brain be annoyed by these things? Irritated? Frustrated?

My sister does cocaine with a cute Mexican to cope with her complicated feelings and sends a string of text messages to the Family Group Text.

My dad's side of the family tree branches throughout West Virginia and some of Kentucky. One of eight—seven boys and a lonely sister who insisted on dressing my dad as a girl when he was an infant—my dad grew up as the next-to-last child and spent most of his time with his younger brother Roger. My sister and I grew up with Roger's kids as if they were our siblings, our own nucleus of private jokes, fights, and unspoken love.

We decide to include two significant others in the Family Group Text.

Why are none of you angry? Sarah texts.

I am fucking angry.

There is a cute Mexican in my bed and we snorted a bunch of coke together.

My dog has been walked, if any of you were wondering.

I tell Sarah to go to bed. I realize, though, telling someone who just did a bunch of coke to go to bed is like telling a small dog to stop yipping and biting at feet.

There are answers out there.

We have to fix this.

It's a conspiracy.

I don't feel sick I don't feel sick I don't feel sick.

Part of brain surgery, part of cancer, part of being sick without feeling sick, is coping with other peoples' feelings, other peoples' reactions, and other peoples' emotions. Understanding that family, friends, and loved ones feel as lost as unnamed stars trying to fix the problems of the galaxy, the sky, the universe. Realizing that they feel even more helpless, scared, and alone than I do.

I can't tell Dad or Sarah, I tell my mom after Dr. Bixton's diagnostic visit. *They are not strong like we are. They do not know how to cope.*

My mom tells my dad and reports back that he *was very brave.*

Sarah did—is doing?—cocaine with a cute Mexican, who is now happily snoring in her bed.

I have not felt angry I have not felt angry I have not felt angry.

My youngest cousin Cathleen sends pictures of her cat, Aladdin, screaming in the bathtub because he has *sepurration anxiety.*

Anything to get Sarah to stop talking about brain tumor conspiracy theories.

Don't let them tell you that you're dying SZ.

We are going to fix this.

Update: the Mexican wants to cuddle. What should I do?

Megan, the first time I saw you play the drums I almost cried because it was mad cute.

I don't feel sick I don't feel angry I don't feel anything.

wake forest baptist hospital, sticht center, the dash

My mother organizes my room at the rehabilitation center one final time before she leaves.

I am ready for her to go; she is ready to go.

My dad has not done well without her. He has not taken his trips to the gym to do the stationary bike, and he has not eaten enough of the pizza, the hamburgers, and snacks that my hometown community has brought him.

Everyone needs my mom.

The cancer (me), the diabetes (me), the Lyme disease (dad): we all need her.

I did not realize how much I needed her until she mentioned leaving a week earlier. I became so upset I cried when she left for the hotel that night.

I never knew I needed my mother.

An independent child, I could not wait to abandon my parents for summer camps, friends' houses, and church sleepovers. I had to learn to give my own insulin injections, though, before I could relish the freedom of leaving home. I hated needles (because needles! No one likes those shitty things), so my dad offered to buy me a Nintendo GameBoy if I learned how to inject myself while at type one diabetes summer camp, the only camp I was allowed to attend before conquering the injection process.

Because doctors.

Because nurses.

Because every other kid there had the same problem I did.

She really wants to learn how to give herself injections, my mom wrote on the summer camp questionnaire.

I did not.

I did not want diabetes at all.

She is a bit scared, but she has expressed the desire to learn.

I suppose my parents wanted that independent child.

After a week in the neurology unit, after the craniotomy, and after a week of intensive rehabilitation, I am ready for independence again.

Because this is love.

Teaching someone to live without you.

wake forest baptist hospital, sticht center, the dash

Anitra wakes me at five a.m. for my bath.

I can wash myself, I tell her.

Okay, Miss Independent, that's not what your chart says.

I do not want anyone to watch me bathe.

I plan to wipe myself off, slap on some deodorant, and be ready for my day: physical therapy, occupational therapy, speech therapy, physical therapy again, and then visitors. I am not permitted to wet my staples, so I cannot wash my hair without Angel's help. Before this, before the cancer bullshit, I washed my hair every morning. Sometimes twice a day, especially after going to the gym.

And now, I have not washed my hair since I last saw Angel. She has been out to stay with her sick son for three days? Four days? Too long.

I feel so dirty.

I feel so ashamed.

I feel like a fucking skuzz.

I feel like a cancer myself: a gross growth inside this hospital that might mold to the wall if I do not escape sometime soon.

Anitra rips off my nightgown and lifts me onto the shower chair.

But I am not getting a shower; I am getting a sponge bath.

Everyone here has seen me naked now.

Some have seen me struggle to insert a tampon with my left hand; some have seen me drink orange juice while attempting to have a bowel movement.

Now Anitra has seen all of me, exposed and pissed off.

Philosophy, she says as she reaches for my shower gel. *Does the church sell this? This is nice. I ain't never seen nothing like this before.*

I do not understand, but I still have armpits, butt, and behind the knees with Anitra.

I don't know, I say. *Some nice friends brought me that.*

I think the church sells that, Anitra says as she scrubs my elbows.

Sure, I say. *I think the church sells that shower gel.*

I want to push Anitra away, turn on the shower, and wash my goddamn hair.

Anitra washes my dry skin with a cold washcloth and hands me my underwear. They are dirty. I put them on anyway.

You're done, she says as she towels off the wet bathroom floor.

I let Anitra help me and my dirty underwear back into my adjustable bed.

I hear the sink dripping but convince myself I am having an auditory hallucination.

When I wake up again an hour later, water has flooded my bathroom floor and there are no rainbows to be seen, no colors lighting my morning, no hope for a brighter afternoon.

wake forest baptist hospital, sticht center, the dash
Rider, my friend and old roller derby teammate, brings me a Mike Tyson shirt and a fresh box of tampons.

I love her.

wake forest baptist hospital, sticht center, the dash
The second time I cry while I am here has nothing to do with me.

This is not to say that I am selfless or without feelings regarding my own diagnosis; I cannot cry about brain cancer, even when I try.

Instead, I watch the life flight helicopters land outside my rehab room. I cannot see, not from the wheelchair, anyway, if the pilot brings people or organs to the hospital, but I always hope for organs.

The second time I cry has everything to do with a little girl admitted to the rehab facility a week before I leave.

I see the girl's Gigi push her around in a wheelchair. Well, no big deal. All of us in the rehab center were or still are in wheelchairs. I had graduated to sometimes using a walker the day before, but we have all given our lives over to that chair, at least for a few weeks.

I cry when I see a tube coming out of the girl's nose. When I realize she can no longer speak and is trying to learn sign language. When I see her carrying around a stuffed penguin on her lap whenever she goes to physical therapy.

My favorite nursing assistant, Linda, comes in while I am crying and says *it's okay, it's just because you care*. It's just because I know this isn't fair; I know this is a shit show circus, and little children should have no part in the production.

I make the little girl a gift from presents people have sent me. The funny thing about brain cancer is that people assume I reverted back to being a child. In a way, I did. I still cannot move my foot or ankle, and I want to wear pajamas all day. Otherwise, I am still the same functioning adult I was before December 18th.

But people have sent me sweet coloring books, sticker books, and stuffed animals. I love these things, and I love the thought behind them. However, I have never liked coloring or sticker books; the stuffed animals have been nice to squeeze at night, nice to keep me company, but I do not need everything: I do not need all of them.

I use a PATIENT BELONGINGS bag—there must be fifty of them smashed into my room's cubby—to prepare the little girl (whose name I later learn is Katie, a name I insisted my swimming teacher at the YMCA call me if I was drowning) a present. She spied me earlier in the small physical therapy gym and let Gigi know that she liked the side bun of my hair.

I never wanted children.

Thank god. That would have been difficult to deal with given the diagnosis.

Anyway.

I prepare her a care package with a checkers game, a coloring book, a sticker book, and a blue stuffed animal. I cannot remember who gave me these things, and I hope they do not mind me sharing. I do not know if

I am allowed to do this—hospitals have weird rules about these sorts of things sometimes—but I take the bag out to the nurses' station and ask them to deliver it.

This is the closest thing to giving someone a Christmas present I have been able to manage this year, although I did Amazon Prime (yes, I made that a verb) Feeney a dinosaur mug that turns the predators to bones when the water gets hot.

I suppose, just like everything else, giving Katie the gift bag has more to do with me than it does with her.

A few hours later, Katie and Gigi visit my room to thank me for the gift. Gigi finds a special, personal connection with each aspect of the gift. She notes that she and Katie have been playing checkers, that sticker books were Katie's *absolute favorite* before *all of this happened*, that when she was younger, Katie and her sister collected miniature blue dolls like the one I gave her.

Gigi has not abandoned Katie's side since they arrived. I do not know if Katie has parents; I assume she does, but maybe they have to work or have other children.

Gigi stays.

She goes to therapy. She watches Katie eat, because that is the only way Katie will consume any nutrition: if Gigi remains.

Gigi smiles and is so friendly to me, but I can see the fear, the hurt, the pain in her blue eyes. Her irises match the subtle ocean color of the gondola painting I have stared at every night for two weeks.

Gigi—*before all this happened*—likely spent her afternoons with a book club or maybe shopping for herself and her grandchildren at department stores. Even during *all of this happening*, Gigi remains thin, blonde, and perfect at mascara application.

Currently, Gigi finds herself distressed because she cannot remember the name of a math professor at Appalachian State, where I teach English. She wonders if we might know one another, but I assure her that I know no one who teaches math. Gigi searches, she looks in a planner, but she finds nothing.

She seems so disappointed in herself. Gigi just wants to make everyone here happy; she just wants to fix us all.

Katie is ready to go.

She pushes her wheelchair out of my room with her good foot. She signs *thank you* to me, and rolls away.

Gigi looks as if she might cry, just as I did earlier, and I wish I could hug her and make everything feel normal again.

nowhere

Having aggressive brain cancer brings out the best in people, the worst.

Most times I sit quietly and wonder what any of this has to do with me.

Most times, the answer is nothing.

I wish I could help, make everyone feel better, make this disappear like a star falling into a canyon, unafraid of where it might go.

wake forest baptist hospital, sticht center, the dash

The only music I listen to in the hospital is Sufjan Stevens' *Carrie and Lowell*.

The only food I order for dinner is salmon, mashed potatoes, and green beans.

The only television show I watch is *Shark Tank*.

The only thing I think about is walking again.

The only thing I read is Sylvia Plath's "Tulips."

I do not feel sick I do not feel sick I do not feel sick.

I cannot focus on anything for longer than 7.2 minutes; I time this.

I miss my cats and my dog more than anything. I want someone to sneak them in, but I am also afraid of my cat Prufrock murdering someone with her two tiny incisors, or at least infecting someone with those bacteria-filled teeth.

I feel stuck I feel stuck I feel stuck.

The only dream I have is in black and white.

The only thing I write is my signature and my letters, still backhanded.

The only juice I drink is cranberry.

The only person I want in my room is my mother.

The only clothes I wear are leggings and sweatpants.

I do not feel sick I do not feel angry I do not feel like I am dying.

wake forest baptist hospital, sticht center

Having cancer is all about other people.

Especially the kind of cancer where you have a high likelihood of dying.

Did you get my package? I sent you eight books on how cancer is a conspiracy theory. And some socks! You're going to be fine. You're going to be just fine, Jesus is with you!

DID YOU GET MY PACKAGE?

I SENT YOU A PACKAGE THREE DAYS AGO ABOUT CANCER CONSPIRACY THEORIES HELLO.

HI JUST CHECKING IN. MY RECORDS SAY PACKAGE DELIVERED?

I HOPE YOU GOT THE PACKAGE JUST LET ME KNOW.

Yes, hello Stephanie, I got your effing package. Do you feel better about yourself now? Do you feel like you helped me beat brain cancer? Well, here's the sad truth. I have not beaten brain cancer. I am right in the middle of it. I may not beat brain cancer. I may fucking die, and there is nothing you can send me that may change that possibility.

Oh and PRAYERS.

What if your prayers do not receive the answer you desire, Stephanie? What if your package of cancer conspiracy books and socks that say *Jesus Loves You!* do not save my body or my soul? What if your package being delivered has nothing to do with my illness?

I do not feel sick I do not feel sick I do not feel sick.

I am not ungrateful, Stephanie. You are very sweet. Your gift was very thoughtful. You desired for me to feel good, to feel better when I opened the package.

I'm so sorry. I just do not have the strength to respond to you right now. Simply tearing the tape off your package makes me feel like I need to nap for an hour. No, I am not kidding. I have no idea if the exhaustion, the fatigue, the tiredness is from the craniotomy or the swelling still present in my brain. I do not know. I just know that I am SO FUCKING TIRED that I cannot respond to your message, your phone call, your persistent insistence that I answer you so you can feel better about my disease.

Yes, I know that I have a chance of beating this.

Yes, I know that your mother's uncle's sister's poodle had a brain tumor that was taken out, biopsied, and determined to be cancerous.

Yes, I know that they transported the dog to Barbados where they are practicing the newest, greatest, most experimental treatments that have been proven to really work.

But all I want to do right now is watch old *America's Next Top Model* episodes until I have to start chemotherapy and radiation in a week. I want to do nothing. I want to feel nothing. I want to be nothing.

Thank you for your prayers.

I am irritable, tired, and want to spend my energy talking to my close friends and family members.

I do not want to be a bitch.

I do not want to be rude.

I do not want to be thankless.

I am just tired; I am just someone recovering from a craniotomy who does not want to be on an electronic device responding to people I haven't heard from for six years.

I do not feel sick I do not feel sick I do not feel sick.

I feel something else entirely.

ARE YOU SURE YOU RECEIVED THE PACKAGE AND NOT YOUR HOSPITAL NEIGHBOR OR SOMETHING? You know a lot of people steal these days!!!!!

Thank you, Stephanie. Thank you.

I appreciate you so much, but I would really just do anything to be at home with my pets right now.

Having cancer is all about you, always.

wake forest hospital, sticht center, the dash

Only the fourth staple hurts coming out of my head. I hear them *click click click* as the nurse drops them onto my dinner tray as if they are tiny chicken bones she accidentally found in her buffet dinner.

wake forest baptist hospital, sticht center, the dash

This is not a Tuesday with Morrie.

This is a Wednesday with Olaf, and he has centered his orthopedic shoe on the breakfast table like an oyster shell. His entire world exists inside this shoe—everything that thrills him, everything that irritates him, and everything that breathes within him lives here. In this vessel, everything that moves within the sea of Olaf's quiet, busy mind shifts and waves above the padded heel.

I marvel at the shoe oyster and wait to see how long the creature can float on the table before the nurse steals the pearl of our morning and forces us to drink Ensure and eat bacon that looks like a dog treat.

I speculate that Olaf had a stroke; Olaf is unlikely to speculate that my 36th birthday gifted me with a surprise, malignant brain tumor, leaving my dominant side paralyzed.

Olaf must wonder, though, why he gets to share his breakfast shoe oyster with a woman half his age, a woman, who in the span of a day, went from playing roller derby to pushing herself around in a wheelchair with her left heel.

Olaf does not trust my youth, but he trusts my silence; I have not outed his shoe oyster to the nurse, so we remain cohorts, soldiers, friends.

As I stare at my soggy raisin bran, Olaf takes a veiny hand and presses on the shelled exterior of the shoe. He is a phrenologist searching for our answers, yet he cannot reveal the results to either of us.

I am jealous of his dexterity, his deft, tactile investigation of the creature. I yearn for his ability to twist the shoelace around the mollusk of our morning, our new normal.

Olaf's brackish eyes brighten as he lifts a small rock from the shoe oyster. The dulled winter sunrise fuzzes through the window, and I wish for water, for the smell of salt.

We have caught something, I think, as the nurse wordlessly tosses our shiny jewel into the sterile trashcan.

nowhere

I have always wanted the opportunity to write without any other work to worry me.

I thought this might happen from a two-dollar Powerball ticket, but instead, brain cancer made this a reality.

Thank you, dear tumor. Thank you for infiltrating my brain with icky glue and giving me the opportunity to hone my voice, to turn my flash fiction into a memoir-ish type of thing.

Would Dave Eggers read this? I hope so. Would Dave Eggers care? I hope not.

My writing is not for everyone.

My writing is not for me.

This is for you, tumor, cancer, headache.

(But only a metaphorical headache. I have not experienced any actual headaches or double vision. My doctors cannot believe this.)

This book is for you.

This book has always been for you.

wake forest baptist hospital, sticht center, the dash
I have the talent for attracting diseases meant for old people.

Brain cancer.

Diabetes.

Those sorts of disorders.

Does this give me an excuse?

No.

Okay, sometimes.

Sometimes I do not want to keep my mouth shut; sometimes I want to scream at people I have disliked for years but am still Facebook friends with just because social media, social norms; sometimes I want to slap Chole's ex, who helped fuck up my last relationship just because she could, just because I want to feel my cold palm on her smug face; sometimes I want to set fire to the woods behind my apartment just because I want to see the beautiful destruction of flaming dry branches and senseless acorns finally end at the roaring river, that water voracious for the detritus of my shock, my sadness, my void.

Sometimes I want someone to blame. This is a normal reaction, I am sure. I do not ask *why*, but I want to understand *why*. I want to understand why this happened to me, a healthy (except for the diabetes thing) woman in my mid-30s who worked out six days a week and drank beer and soda occasionally but tried to stick with water and love and health.

Sometimes I want to stop people from telling me *I am so strong, I am so fierce*. People who do not see me say these words, write these words. They feel confident I *can do this, beat this*. I know they mean well, but I do not always believe them. I want to sleep, I want to close my eyes and hope to wake up.

John McCain, Beau Biden, 70-year-old men at the rehab center, my high school principal.

These are people with my type of cancer.

I do not often ask why because I would rather know how.

How the fuck did this happen? How did I wake up one morning with a goddamn brain tumor?

The foot, the numbness, the inability for me to move quickly enough. The hard time standing up from the table. That just happened once. The two falls in one day. I am just clumsy, yes.

I do not feel sick I do not feel sick I do not feel sick.

I consider the signs and symptoms as I eat my omelet with men twice my age. They stare at me as if I have stolen something from them, as if I am a blood clot in their brains, a tumor myself.

I suppose I understand.

What I do not understand: how this happened.

It's nothing I did or did not do, my chemo doctor tells me when we meet. Yes, there is a chemo oncologist and a radiation oncologist. Not a singular oncologist. One for each treatment. Then there is a neurologist, a surgeon, a this, a that.

I never dream about the doctors together, all sitting around a table and wondering how they might cure me, but maybe one day I will.

wake forest baptist hospital, sticht center, the dash

Are you the type of woman who does laundry? an elderly man asks me over breakfast. *My wife won't do mine, and I'm looking for someone new. I think that someone might be you.*

wake forest baptist university, sticht center, the dash

Karen, my recreation therapist, takes me to a bookstore.

I have not been outside since December 18, and now it's nearly the middle of January. I struggle to navigate the bumpier terrain with my walker and move slowly so I do not fall. I get into Karen's car and marvel at all the people in the parking lot and on the sidewalk as we drive. I have not seen people; I have not been outside; I have not seen birds or trees or the glaring threats of consumerism for a month.

Look, there's a hawk, Karen says as she points.

I panic because she does not have two hands on the wheel.

I imagine that the hawk is my Uncle Roger. He died from lung cancer two years ago and adopted the hawk as a symbol of his successes throughout the disease.

Someone without a pass has taken over the bookstore's only handicap spot.

Dangit, Karen says. *Happens all the time.*

Once inside, I wander through the aisles and shelves with passionate intensity. I browse through my old friends: Wordsworth, Woolf, Eggers, and Plath.

Do you remember me? I ask. Do you remember who I am?

I think they remember.

I think that they do.

wake forest baptist hospital, sticht center, the dash

Maya, the newest CNA, decides to put Olaf to bed at 7:00 p.m.

No one stops her.

He is tired and asks to rest.

I've gotten to know Maya; I was there for her first overnight shift and her subsequent shifts since then. She is young, maybe just turned 18, and desperately wants to please her patients and her superiors. She kindly wraps the blood pressure cuff around my arm at 3:00 a.m. and has cute, alliterative names for everything.

Squishy socks.

Fuzzy feets.

Cuppy cups.

When my period mysteriously comes back after three days of finishing, she makes me feel normal for getting blood all over my new underwear that my mom sent from Amazon Prime.

Oh, that happened to me the other day! That really sucks, doesn't it?
She might be my favorite.
Sure, this is only her third night, but she cares. I know she cares.
I can tell she cares.

wake forest baptist hospital, sticht center
I cannot decide if I am more like an elderly person or a baby.
I get food all over my sleeve when I attempt to eat: both.
I did not want my mom to leave me: baby.
Most of my conversations are about weather: elderly.
Sometimes I just want people to leave me alone: elderly.
Sometimes I just want someone to hold me or pet my head and tell me I will be okay: baby.
I cannot decide if I am going to die a painful, pitiful death or somehow make it out of this alive, okay, together.

wake forest baptist hospital, sticht center, the dash
It was the fucking aspartame.
There is no other answer.
This type of thing only happens to me late at night. When I am alone. Evenings when I cannot fathom how I am likely going to die soon and alone and without anyone holding my hand. I do not want anyone to pity me, or maybe I do. No. I wish to die with someone I love touching my skin, telling me not to fear the unknown, but if anyone did, it would be a sham. No one loves me right now; this is just not how it all worked out. Sure, a ton of people care; a ton of people wish to send me socks, to mail me cards.
But no one will be with me in those final terrifying moments.
And according to my doctor and the internet, those moments will occur within a year, maybe just a little bit longer.
So after some research, I determine that this diagnosis, this

occurrence, must have happened because of the fucking aspartame.

Katharine Halbert from middle school warned me of this. With her long, unwashed mud-colored hair, Katharine preached to me about how her parents researched what happened to mice when they ate too much aspartame, and they all—all of them—died from cancer. Some type of cancer, any type of cancer, every type of cancer.

I drank roughly seven Diet Mountain Dew cans per day throughout middle school and high school.

I mean, I had type one diabetes. I did not have much of a choice. Maybe seven was a bit too many, a bit extreme. But I did not drink or eat any sugar, except when my parents went to bed and I snuck packets of candy into my bedroom and crunched on old Halloween Sweet Tarts and hoped that no one could hear.

I could not stand Katharine Halbert. She wanted me to die. She wanted me to die, so I wrote her a fake love letter from a boy who did not exist. I did this because I wanted things to be fair, to be just. Katharine Halbert was, and probably still is, smart. Too smart to believe a teenage boy named Mitchell Horchung believed her to be beautiful, to be intelligent, to be *just perfect for him under a galaxy full of stars, comets, and objects shinier than engagement rings.*

Oh, Katharine Halbert.

You really need to quit drinking that stuff. It's going to kill you, just like those mice.

I didn't have a choice, Katharine Halbert.

Maybe she was trying to warn me, to save me, to be nice. Maybe her *don't drink that shit, my parents discovered it gives mice cancer* speech was to help me out. Sure, the whole soliloquy felt stilted and self-righteous and smug, but maybe I should have given her more credit.

I wanted to see the cure for type one diabetes in my lifetime.

I never cared much for cancer.

It was the Diet Mountain Dew cans, it was the fake sugar, it was the aspartame.

I did myself in.

I wonder if Katharine Halbert kept that fake letter from Mitchell Horchung.

I wonder if a small part of her hoped that the letter was real, was honest, was something she could look forward to coming true.

Like a cancer diagnosis from too much aspartame.

It was the fucking aspartame.

wake forest baptist hospital, sticht center, the dash

I stand and hug Linda, my favorite nursing assistant.

I stand on my own.

I had no idea how small she was.

Until now, I had never been standing with her in the room. I had always been in the wheelchair or in the bed or on the toilet.

I will miss Linda and her white tights.

I will miss Linda and her soft finger sticks.

I will miss the people who care.

wake forest baptist hospital, sticht center, the dash

Hours before I leave the Sticht Center, I finish my masterpiece: a sticker artwork of Beyoncé that I give to the receptionist for her birthday.

Now that took some patience, I hear her tell the nurses. *Now that took some patience.*

preheating

wake forest baptist hospital, sticht center, the dash/boone, north carolina

Nodya, my best friend from graduate school, and her husband pick me up from the rehab center to take me home. I use a walker to hobble toward the car as they pack my suitcase and belongings into the vehicle. I almost fall on my way out; the rocky sidewalks pose a problem for someone accustomed to flat, sterile floors.

What do you want to eat? they ask me.

I want fucking Bojangles.

Bojangles is a fast food chicken and biscuits restaurant that rivals any Southern grandmother's kitchen. I want nothing more than to stuff my face with fried chicken, seasoned fries, and a buttery biscuit.

That's the most gangster thing I've ever heard, my friend's husband says.

I am quiet for the two-hour drive home. Once we arrive, one cat rubs against my legs, thrilled to see me, while the other hides behind the water heater and hisses.

We all have our ways of dealing with disasters.

Nodya and I clean the inside of the apartment while her husband begins making me a handicapped-accessible entrance to my apartment.

Before: mud.

After: a nice sidewalk I can actually navigate.

Everything has changed. Everything is different. I am no longer the same, but I am thankful for people who understand this, the people who offer their lives to help me live my own.

boone, north carolina

JC sends me some sugarless, aspartame-less energy drinks and dog treats through Amazon Prime.

The notes come from her dog.

ENERGY WATER CURE HAHA.

JC lives twenty minutes from me.

Her dog finds great joy in online shopping.

boone, north carolina

I collapse onto Chris's arm as we drive to my apartment from Starbucks.

I cry.

I haven't cried much.

This is what happens when I feel comfortable.

You can cry whenever you want, she says. *You can cry whenever you need to.*

But I can't, not even when I try.

nowhere

I wish I could touch my brain.

I wish I could manipulate the Brain Glue Gone Wild—that's basically what a glioblastoma is—and pull it out of there. I would put all of that Brain Glue Gone Wild into a Mason jar and stare at the substance before falling asleep.

I would study that glue and then tightly close the jar so none could escape, so none could crawl back where it certainly never belonged.

If I could pull a chunk of my skull out whenever I felt the urge and then swipe out that Glue Gone Wild anytime the substance appeared, I could save myself. I could heal myself. I could prevent anything else bad from happening to my most precious landmark, my most coveted possession, my favorite place to rest.

I could then pop the chunk of my skull back onto my head like a missing puzzle piece, and no one would know that anything had happened, that anything was wrong, that anything went awry at all.

boone, north carolina

Late at night, I think about how no one has ever been in love with me.

I hate these self-absorbed thoughts. I think about Morrissey singing *there are things worse in life than never being someone's sweetie.* This is true, of course. There are so many sick people, so many children dying, so many people without families or homes. But does this discount my sadness? What qualifies me to have or not have these thoughts? Is the deadly combination of type one diabetes and brain cancer enough? Is brain cancer enough on its own? Is any of this enough to grant me a few moments to feel sorry for myself about *the right people* never falling in love with me?

Chole would say no, but we fucking hate Chole.

All of us.

People tried to fall in love with me, but they weren't the right ones. Perhaps this makes me seem even more self-absorbed and trite, but no— it would have never worked. These two people I am considering did not understand my mind, did not understand why I had no interest in adopting a miniature pinscher or reading Harry Potter books all day long.

It would have never worked.

Neither of them.

I did them a favor, right? They both moved on to have successful, happy relationships with other people, and I found myself happy for them, quite pleased for their romantic trajectories, their soaring leaps into a love far beyond what I could provide.

You have tons, so many people who care about you, Chris tells me. She runs a near-death experience website, and I am sure she will add a testimonial of mine on there after I'm gone. I hope she uses the recent nightmare I had where I was dying, I was alone, there was blackness, and I felt like I was going to vomit up the Thin Mints Girl Scout Cookies I inhaled after brushing my teeth. *Everyone cares about you.*

But no one cares enough about me to hold my hand when I die. This is a right reserved for people in love, for people who have made that promise to one another. A right reserved for all the cancer movies out there. This right does not necessarily mean marriage, but a commitment that they would be there, dammit, and love the other person until the breath left their body in a light blue cloud of finality and peace.

I am not part of anyone's daily life, I tell Chris. *No one but two cats and a dog wake up to me. And I will find them new homes, new moms. Except Pru, who will need to be euthanized once I die, because no one can deal with that. She barely survived my weeks in the hospital.*

Chris does not like what I have said.

You mean to say that you wouldn't be sad if I died? If Rolli died? If Jenna died?

Of course I would be sad.

Devastated.

You will all move on because you all have someone to move on with, I say. *You might not forget about me immediately, but you will. Eventually. At some point, it will be like I was never there at all.*

I do not say this to make Chris, or anyone, feel sorry for me. I believe these words to be true. Sure, my friends and family will miss me, especially the first two or three weeks after I am gone, but soon enough, they will leave the house again. They will meet new people. They will drink high-percentage beer at the local brewing company and laugh in the bracingly cold moonlight while some terrible 90s cover band fucks up the words to "Semi-Charmed Life." They will forget about me until they stumble home alone and scroll through Instagram pictures and find one with me smiling, smiling, smiling and them clutching my arm because I had no idea that I was about to get fucking brain cancer at 36-years old—but maybe something inside of them predicted I would not be around forever or as long as they would have liked. Their stomachs will knot in regret and longing for a brief moment before they fall asleep and wake up the next morning to rush to work, to respond to unanswered text messages, to eat a granola bar and head to the gym to work off those 140 calories because goddammit, they need to be healthy and live forever.

I did all those things, too.

Sometimes I forget I am not yet dead.

Sometimes I speak about myself in the past tense already.

Sometimes I feel I might die before treatments even start, my head buzzing with new cancer cells ready to form, divide, and take over my brain, my body, my life in a spread of dark, sad entities no one ever loved or recognized.

This is just how death works, I tell Chris. *Everyone eventually forgets. They have to.*

You're on the other side, she says. *You're never going to understand.*

But Chris is not in love with me; no one is, and I cannot make anyone decide on me or even take me on as a pity project to give me some happiness before the end disallows me to speak, feel, or return love.

The loneliness pervades my skin, my body; the isolation pumps through my veins and competes with those cancer cells, with those aggressive, shitty killers who want nothing more than to end my life.

I do not feel sick I do not feel sick I do not feel sick.

I only feel alone.

wake forest baptist hospital, office visit, the dash
To participate in the chemo clinical trial my doctor has recommended, I must have my heart examined.

My heart stays busy applauding itself, clapping for its good work.

The heart was never the problem, and it knows this.

My heart knows how well she has done, how many days, hours, minutes she has kept me alive, awake, alert. Thriving. Way to go, you fucking badass, she says to herself on the echocardiogram. Way to fucking go. You did it, you bitch. While the pancreas and brain were sleeping and taking breaks whenever they pleased, you carried on and kept this body moving.

I like to tell people that their hearts are praising God, the ultrasound technician tells me. *Praising God for a job well done.*

I do not know how to respond to this, so I say nothing.

Doctors like to rule everything out, he says. *They start with three things, but I think they always suspect a number one. If it's not number one, they go to number two. Then number three. Process of elimination.*

I want to tell him how there is nothing left to rule out; I have brain cancer. Everyone knows and understands this.

I have brain cancer.

My tumor is also MGMT negative, which means I do not have the protein that responds well to Temodar, the type of chemo I was supposed to take before the clinical trial arrived.

But the clinical trial.

The new medication I will take is called BAL101553.

Or something like that.

These medical acronyms and number lists do not translate well for English professors. MGMT is a band I listened to when I was married, a long time ago. Now they're are a bit too peppy for me, a bit twee, but whatever.

But presently, MGMT is some sort of gene, some sort of protein my tumor lacks.

This is neither good nor bad, really, not at this point.

The lack of MGMT means I will have a place in a clinical trial that utilizes a different type of chemotherapy that may be more effective? Perhaps? No one is terribly sure quite yet; no one really knows.

I'm sure this is the fun of a clinical trial: something new, something different, something unknown.

The radiation tech does not have an accent, so I know he is from near where I grew up. This is how I tell; I start with three things. If they don't have an accent, I rule out that they are from the South. If they don't discuss college basketball, I rule out that they are from North Carolina.

It's the discussion of God that has me troubled.

I'm from Ohio, he tells me, as if the echocardiogram has also allowed him to read minds.

Near the Marietta area, I guess.

How did you know?

My heart valves click, they flail, they clap.

I know because I recognize his voice. I do not know him, not really, but I do. He is every middle-aged man from greater Appalachia whose accent does not have a place to call home.

So you start chemo soon, he says. I know he wants to proselytize me; I know he wants to say more. *Drink your greens, eat healthy. I'll be praying for you, for sure.*

Job well done, my ventricles say. Job well done.

nowhere

I don't have a karaoke song, but if I did, it would be The Divinyls, "I Touch Myself."

It's a highly underrated song.

physical therapy center, boone, north carolina

When I leave the hospital, I can walk without a walker or wheelchair. I wear an air cast on my right ankle and a "foot up" brace that forces my toes to leave the floor when I stride. This prevents me from dragging my foot like a deer that's been run over but refuses to die.

Now I am in the wild, the wilderness, the woods.

I still take the walker on excursions. Uneven terrain—even just the slight jut of a rock or cracked concrete—causes me to fear for my safety, to fear I might fall like an elderly person and break a hip, to fear I might trip over a rug or a carpet or an unexpected table leg and cause myself to need another surgery of some sort.

People stare, of course. Bathrooms are difficult; even the accessible restrooms have a door, and managing a door, a walker, and an uncooperative body is an effort worthy of a two-hour nap.

People refuse to move a little forward, a little backward, a little to the side. They likely believe I have a sports injury or am just clumsy. Still, after an SUV nearly flattens me like Roland Barthes, I begin to see just how often people are assholes to the differently abled.

For instance: a woman I will call Carol.

I do not know her.

I do not know her actual name.

She wears no nametag or monogrammed materials.

She just looks like a Carol.

Before one of my physical therapy appointments in Boone, I pull myself into the waiting room and struggle to find a place to sit that will accommodate both myself and the walker. I carefully choose the chair across from Carol because I can a) sit in the chair and b) put my walker in the side space without disturbing anyone.

This displeases Carol.

She stares at me.

Carol rolls her eyes.

She huffs. She puffs. She wants to blow my walker down with her untamed, wolfish eyebrows.

I HAVE FUCKING BRAIN CANCER CAROL.

I do not say this, but I feel as if Carol reads my thoughts. She stands up—without any assistance from a cane, walker, or other device—and struts to a new seat closer to the doors.

BYE CAROL.

Sure, I understand. I am 36, but I look younger. (When visiting me in the hospital, one of my friends asks if my mother was a teen mom. *She looks so young*, she says. My mom had me when she was 27, but she very much appreciates the compliment. I appreciate the genes. My type of tumor, a glioblastoma multiforme, is not hereditary, and most current research does not credit family history for type one diabetes. I have no one to blame for those. What I'm trying to say is *thank you, Mom. Thank you.*) I have been doing everything to make myself look presentable: wearing makeup, putting on clean clothes, owning my half-shaved head as I have for the past two years I've had the haircut.

Carol does not appreciate my attempts.

I also appear, perhaps, as if I can function without my walker. I can, mostly. It's the *mostly* I fear—what if I drag my lame foot behind me *just once* and trip? What if that trip causes me to break my ankle or dislocate my knee? Carol did not witness my vacation to the bathroom where I left the walker outside of the stall and almost fell because the lights were off, and I could not find the switch.

I felt weightless, as if I was floating in space. I needed to find a comet, a star, a planet: something warm I could grasp.

I located the light switch and steadied myself with the vanity table. I knocked off a potpourri container and retrieved the leaves from the floor.

A flower girl in reverse.

I have become quite good at bending my knees.

Carol does not see this.

I HAVE BRAIN CANCER CAROL.

I do not know how this happened, Carol. No one does. Not me, not my family, not my friends, not my doctor.

Shit happens, Carol.

I do not know what happened to you, Carol, but it must have been bad. Or maybe you have no support. No friends, no family left to help you. I don't know, but I do not assume. I am not like you, Carol.

I am unlike the bad thoughts in your head.

I am not sick I am not sad I am not angry.

Please do not be angry, Carol. Please do not be angry.

boone, north carolina

My sister Sarah comes to stay with me for a month so she can take me to radiation treatments. I am not permitted to drive because of the seizures; I cannot move my right foot yet, so I could not drive if I wanted to. Sarah finds a friend to sublet her Williamsburg studio and her salon booth.

She orders a cabbie hat from Amazon because she takes her role as my chemo and radiation driver very seriously.

Sarah does not take herself very seriously.

When the hat arrives, she commits to the fashion and wears the accoutrement around the apartment all afternoon.

Beep. Vroom. Honk.

My sister is a terrible driver.

She car dances. She texts and drives. She drinks iced coffee and spits it all over the steering wheel while she sings the gypsy music of our ancestors, of our long-lost mothers and fathers.

wake forest baptist hospital, office visit, the dash

I can't believe you are walking, Dr. Bixton, my surgeon, the Man with the Briefcase says.

I am walking. I still have the air cast and foot brace, but I am walking. I have difficulty standing up from chairs, but I can. These hardships increase when my blood sugar is too high or low.

But I am walking.

You don't even have your walker.

I can't believe you are walking.

You are doing phenomenal. I would have never said this, but I didn't think you would walk again.

I smile. I cross my feet, just because I can. I tell my surgeon how my foot moved at physical therapy last week.

I am really fucking depressed.

I cannot tell my surgeon this, but he knows.

You've been through some trauma. You are human. You will need to recover mentally from this, and it might take some time. Don't push yourself too hard.

But what if I recover and this all begins again? What if I don't recover? What if the tumor returns, and you all expect me to restart this process of surgery, rehabilitation, chemo, and radiation? What if?

I do not ask these questions.

I do not always want to know the answers.

nowhere

I wonder what would have happened if I had visited a phrenologist in the middle of the Victorian era, maybe somewhere in London or a nearby village.

I imagine popping into a corset storefront and plodding my way through a secret bookshelf door (because this is my Victorian England, dammit), where a pseudoscientist would sit waiting for me, her hands ready to examine my skull, my cranium, my brain for any abnormalities or disfigurements.

She would press her bare fingers onto my forehead and notice the *elevation of benevolence* and *an indentation of reasoning, causality, planning.* The phrenologist would express her concern over this, tell me that *perhaps there is some abnormality there, but you are very kind and giving to those around you.*

Much like a modern psychic or fortune teller, the phrenologist would charge me more than a doctor and invite me to return weekly so she could further enlighten me regarding how to factor this abnormality into my life. She would check for further indentations and elevations to ensure I was sound of mind and character, especially if I needed a job recommendation from her or something of the sort.

I would ride my bicycle to her phrenology den weekly, at least, and read a penny dreadful beside the bookshelf until she was ready for my appointment. I would run out of money for bread and soup ingredients and wish for conversations with Oscar Wilde about his creative process. I would rely on her diagnoses and prognoses until the continual numbness of my right leg would eventually prevent me from riding my bicycle to her secret den.

The phrenologist would begin making visits to my house, but she would charge me more to push her knuckles into my skull, to relieve the pressure above my left eye. She would ask me how I felt, and I would respond

I don't feel sick I don't feel sick I don't feel sick.

After my death, the phrenologist would scalpel out my skull to keep for her records. She would explain to new clients how she kept me alive for much longer than the world wanted, for much longer than anyone expected. She would point to my head as a paragon of her success, as proof of her scientific exploration and discovery.

She would tap my cranium.

She would push.

She would search for any foreign objects that could have diminished my agreeableness, my intuition.

There was something there; there was something new, something that did not belong.

taking poison,
getting my brain microwaved

novant health, office visit, the dash

I see my endocrinologist—my diabetes doctor—a week after my hospital release.

What the hell happened to you?

He asks this in a caring way.

Not accusatory.

He appears stunned.

People with type one diabetes tend to hate their endocrinologist, or at least feel indifferent to the advice and any well-meaning intentions the doctor might have. For those like myself, a person who has had type one diabetes for 31 years, we tend to believe we know more than the endocrinologist, especially one like mine who is around my age, maybe just a few years older, and likely graduated after I had already experienced two-and-a-half decades of the disease.

But I like him. I always have. Most of the time.

He is the first out of my five endocrinologists that I have trusted. The others acted as if they knew too much, tried to prescribe me particular types of insulin because they got monetary or vacation kickbacks, or creepily put me on birth control pills when I explained thoroughly that I was not sexually active.

The others did not make eye contact or see me as a person.

You look really good, he says. *Actually, better than you looked last time.*

I had a crying spell in his office during my last visit. I could make excuses— I was about to start my period, I had a brain tumor in my frontal lobe and had no idea, I was stressed over diabetes control—but the reality was just that I hated diabetes so much that I wanted it to end and be over. Diabetes dominated my life: blood sugar checks, wild glucose swings, and constant monitoring and wondering if a low blood sugar would kill me in my sleep.

Upon leaving, the receptionist said she *would pray for me.*

Thank you.

But this was all before you, tumor, before your cancerous monstrosities invaded my most vital organ.

I was aggressive with your management before, my doctor says. *Perhaps too aggressive. I wanted your averages in the low 100s. But with a lower life expectancy, we can be much less aggressive. Your A1C is 8.3, and that's good. Good enough. Let's keep it between 8 and 9.*

A lower life expectancy.

He is giving me my first free pass with diabetes.

Loosen up, he's telling me. Live your goddamn life. All that is left of it. Don't worry so much; I will not be as hard on you.

I ask him if I can reconnect my insulin pump.

The hospital made me disconnect my pump and revert to injections. Since beginning insulin pump therapy in July, my blood sugar had evened and allowed me to feel more in control. I felt healthier, livelier. Unless I messed up the infusion site, high blood sugars were a past annoyance, something I could look back on nostalgically with frequent pissing and endless cups of lukewarm water.

No, he says. *We can't really have you on the pump because of potential seizure risks.*

I do not quite understand what this means; I know I am on medication to prevent seizures on my lame right side, but I do not comprehend how this might affect my insulin pump.

Okay, I say. *Just please put me on more effective insulin.*

The hospital insisted on giving me insulin I had not taken since 2012, six years earlier. And then they wondered why nothing worked, why I had terrible blood sugars, why I could not get my shit together.

Of course, he says as he briefly touches my leg. His touch does not feel weird; his touch feels more like something someone told him to do in medical school to better his bedside manner. For some reason, it works.

I'm really sorry, he says. *I'm really, really sorry.*

It's okay, I say as I smile.

I know I do not have to smile, but I do. This is, always has been, my natural reaction. A big, bright smile. Never a fake, just a response.

You didn't deserve this, he says. *You look really good.*

Since my diagnosis and surgery, so many people have told me I *look good*. I have spent some time thinking about what this means. What should someone with brain cancer look like? Should I be completely weak, crying all the time, or a bag of disheveled blood vessels and bones? Should I have kept using the wheelchair I depended on at the rehab center? Should I stop listening to true crime podcasts and cease depending on Sylvia Plath's "Tulips" to get me through the day? Should I make sad, wilting posts to Facebook about how I am most likely going to die within the year?

This is not me.

Of course I look good.

Thank you, I say as I walk out of his office. I use the walker but not really. It kind of just sits there for stability purposes. It is snowing outside, after all.

Can I ask what happened? questions the receptionist, the same one who said she would pray for me after my last visit.

The rules of the rehabilitation center—especially the rule where no one questions what happened—do not apply here at the endocrinologist.

I have brain cancer, I announce without quieting my voice.

She turns the same shade as my discharge papers. I can immediately tell she wishes she would have never asked. She was expecting a *oh, I broke my ankle playing adult dodgeball* or *I slipped on the darned ice and sprained my foot*.

I HAVE BRAIN CANCER.

I HAVE BRAIN FUCKING CANCER.

Oh, sweetie, she says, *but you look so good*.

wake forest baptist hospital, comprehensive cancer center, the dash

Currently, I am the only new research patient.

One came before me.

I am not certain what happened to the other patient, who they are, or if the research trial assisted them in any way. I do not know if they were also young and rare, or if they were the typical older male, the John McCain, the Ted Kennedy, the Beau Biden.

I know, I know, Beau Biden was not that old, but he was still older than I am and still male and still all the things one should be before receiving a diagnosis of glioblastoma.

I only know I am the new brain cancer research patient, and here I am.

This means I am a priority.

I have a special room on the fourth floor of the cancer center where I wait for the nurses to take my blood every two hours. They need my blood for some type of evidence, for some type of proof regarding how well the new drug works.

Or how well the new drug does not work.

They will know by my results; I will know by whether I survive.

Before the research nurses show me to the special room, I sit in the downstairs holding deck.

I have completed my first round of radiation.

I don't feel like doing it today, the elderly lady beside me states before I enter the radiation room to have my brain zapped. *I just don't think I'll do my radiation. I'm tired.*

I do not ask the lady how many days she has been coming for radiation, but I know she must be in the teens or twenties. She does not feel like continuing or moving forward with her treatments. Perhaps she does not feel like continuing moving forward with her life.

I would understand.

I will understand.

The radiation technicians play "Tears of a Clown" during my first treatment.

I feel as if I have one lobe of my brain in the future and one in the past. The future brain lobe takes the radiation zaps and morphs them into swords to fight aliens, while the past lobe sits in a diner and listens to songs on a jukebox that is too pink for me but still produces enjoyable music.

The radiation dries out my mouth.

And perhaps my body—afterward, no one could get blood from my veins.

You're dehydrated.

Your veins are too small.

Have they always been like this?

The nurses try different gauges. They attempt IVs and butterfly needles. They dig around in my arm as if they are following a treasure map. However, there is no trunk full of red coins; there is no payoff for the nurses' search.

Just a clear, empty tube.

This is proof, I think.

Proof I already have nothing left to give.

wake forest baptist hospital, comprehensive cancer center, the dash

Punchy, one of the chemo research nurses, tells my sister and me about the wonderful food in the cafeteria.

You can get sandwiches, soups, salads, yogurts, anything you want! she says. *I never get bored with it.*

My sister and I only have 45 minutes before the nurses need to draw my blood again, so Punchy agrees to lead us to the cafeteria so we don't get lost. We follow her through the maze of hospital hallways that are a labyrinth of sterility and lacquered hope.

Instead of taking us to the main cafeteria, Punchy takes us to the Chick-Fil-A that remains separate from the main cafeteria.

This is where you will be eating today, she says as she points toward the abbreviated menu of quick sandwiches and nuggets.

Sarah and I do not look at one another because we know we will laugh.

We just know.

wake forest baptist hospital, office visit, comprehensive cancer center, the dash

Things I did not know: cancer patients have seven thousand doctors. Okay, that's hyperbole. But a lot of doctors. One for chemo, one for radiation, one for surgery, one for whatever the patient has surgery on.

For example, my brain.

A neurosurgeon.

A neurologist.

A radiation oncologist.

A chemo oncologist.

My chemo oncologist, Dr. Stroupe, cares. He is preternaturally kind, which one would expect all doctors to be. They are not, of course, but Dr. Stroupe is. He waits. He listens. He remembers my sister drove all the way from Brooklyn to stay with me and care for me during treatment.

When he walks into the research room and sees me typing on my laptop, he assumes I am surfing the internet.

When I tell him I'm writing a book about *this*, this brain surgery, this cancer diagnosis, this malarkey, he stops before leaving the special patient research room.

Of course you are in the book, I say.

You all are.

Every single one of you.

His face matches the shade of the biohazard warning on the sharps container. Because he is kind, he is worried. Worried he might not be doing a good enough job, though he is. Worried I might make him seem like a jerk, which I would never, unless he was actually a pompous asshole, which he is not.

Part of me wants to speculate: I want to imagine that after long days of dealing with destitute (but smiling!) patients like myself who have brain cancer, he goes home to a brunette wife and twin boys who have little league games on Thursday nights and soccer practice each

Wednesday and every other Sunday. I want to speculate that he has no religious beliefs but admires *the good in all people*, though he may be a Buddhist if pressed or questioned too many times.

Sometimes, he wears his wedding ring on his right hand. At first, I wonder if he is widowed, but then I notice he writes with his left hand. Perhaps I am overthinking his personal life and this is nothing more than a matter of comfort and practicality.

He later tells me *my wife is a dermatologist. She's the smart one in the relationship.*

He is a creative doctor. He writes on the paper that lines the awkward office beds. He makes doodles about the clinical trial I am part of, and then he rips the bed paper off, scrunches the trash into a ball roughly the size of my tumor, and tosses the paper tumor into the trashcan.

Swoosh.

He is just really nice.

He believes in the greater good, whatever that may be.

Because I have basically already killed myself in my sick mind, he attempts to give me hope. He finds me an antidepressant that works well with my chemo treatment so I do not become more ill than necessary. He shakes my hand vigorously and checks on me while I sit in the research room, writing this book, trying to feel as if I am not a randomized patient in a randomized room in a randomized place that is too sterile, too white, too organized for my normal life, my style, my business of being alive.

I like you, Dr. Stroupe. I like your nurses. You are a good man. You are a champion. You are maybe going to save me from the things I cannot yet see.

target, the dash

I take an Uber to Target after a radiation treatment. I am staying at The Hawthorne Hotel because it is supposed to snow in Boone, and I cannot miss any treatments.

I need some things, some things I forgot.

The Target cashier believes I am going on a vacation.

I play along.

Sunglasses

Lip gloss

Mascara

Fancy water bottle

Bikini-style underwear

A dress

A backpack

Two tank tops

I didn't actually make a list; I just started finding things I liked. Not things I needed. Just items I wanted because I found them pretty or thought they would make me pretty or believed they would look pretty on me.

I feel so ugly.

Are you going on a cruise? the cashier asks.

Yes, I say. *Jamaica. I've never been.*

That part is true.

Oh, honey, I've known about three people who have gone down there this time of year. Beautiful. Best time to go. Not a lot of tourists there in February. A lot of people wait until summer.

I can't wait, I say. *I've been looking forward to the trip for about a year.*

You should have gotten yourself a bathing suit! We got some real cute ones over there.

Brain cancer doesn't need a bathing suit, but brain cancer needs sunglasses so I can avoid eye contact in Ubers; brain cancer needs a water bottle so the phlebotomists can suck me dry without a problem; brain cancer needs a backpack because my coordination remains so terrible that I cannot carry a purse without falling over to one side; brain cancer needs tank tops because they actually let me keep those on during radiation; brain cancer needs fancy underwear because I am staying the weekend in The Dash since I'm nauseous, exhausted, and Boone is covered in snow and I cannot miss any treatments; brain cancer needs mascara and lip gloss just because it does, dammit.

I have too many bathing suits already, I say.

At least you got to do some fun shopping!

I do not feel sick I do not feel sick I do not feel sick.

The cashier cannot see my leg, so she assumes I am healthy. I have a toboggan on because it's cold and because I know people can see my sunburned scar on my shaved head. I am without my walker or a wheelchair.

I am free. I am spending money. I am on vacation, right now.

Sometimes I imagine the radiation machine is a sturdy beach towel, and I am at Coney Island. The flashes of light become the July New York sun, and I am happy to burn on the beach. When the radiation table moves, I picture myself on the Ferris wheel with my sister, staring at the hopeful skyline from the swinging car. My radiation mask, the protective layer, keeps everyone safe from falling onto the concrete like splattered pigeons.

I can tell the cashier judges my spending. Who has the money to blow on vacation water bottles? On mascara purchased specifically for Jamaica? Who has multiple bathing suits at home but still wants to spend money on underwear instead of just washing what they already have?

I am not going to Jamaica.

No one is going to Jamaica.

I see contempt hiding in the wrinkles of her face. Here she is, working at Target on her feet all day, while some young lady purchases too many items for an extravagant vacation. How dare I? How dare I show up to this Target and purchase too many items no one should really need or even want?

That fucking fancy water bottle.

I'll think of you when I'm on the beach! I say as I struggle to pick up my bags and exit the checkout line.

I will think of my Judy, my lovely Target cashier, while I am on radiation table one, the Coney Island of Wake Forest Baptist Hospital, baking on the beach and riding the Ferris Wheel while wearing my new sunglasses, too pretty, too carefree.

the hawthorne hotel, the dash

I dance alone in my hotel room.

I recognize my luck; I am not in the hospital, I have no IVs, and I am away from anyone and anything that could possibly bother me.

My sister remains at my apartment in Boone; she must babysit my pets and keep the apartment safe from freezing pipes.

I turn music on and move. I watch myself in the mirror and attempt to match the swing, the pop of each hip, each shoulder, each thigh: one side with the other, exact replicas.

My right side betrays me. I feel as if I am performing similar movements, left then right, but the mirror reveals the truth. My right arm and hip lag behind like a parade mistake; it does not matter how much I feel that I am completing the same movements.

I am wrong.

My right hip does not raise as high as my left, and my right shoulder sinks further below my neck, below my chin, than my left. I am only the marionettist of my left side; my right side is too lame, too tired, too weak.

I remind myself that as a former national champion baton twirler and competitive roller derby skater, I might have been one of the most coordinated people in America. To impress my coach and teammates, I would perform cartwheels on my quad skates. I landed every single time. I never fell or failed.

And now I am a sad, broken puppet; my right side reminds me I am now nothing more than a body half in the past and half in the future. My right side may never catch my left, and I may forever try to force my body to meet somewhere in the middle of my sternum so I can stabilize myself enough to move forward.

My left leg bearing most of my weight, I raise my arms in a pathetic shimmy. How can I be so out of sync with myself?

I wonder. I watch. I wait.

The first time I attempted to walk in the hospital, a physical therapist stopped by the neurology floor. He placed a mirror in front of me and made me watch myself attempt to stride. I did not want to make eye contact with myself; I was too embarrassed to recognize how *unable* I had become. I could once roller skate through three-hour derby practices with minimal water breaks, and now I could not even put one foot in front of the other without skates on my feet.

At the rehabilitation center, Bentley taught me to stand up straight. He showed me how to tuck my ass under my hips and look up, look forward. When the mirror reappeared, I had no choice but to face myself and who I had become. I did not like the present SZ, I did not enjoy this new, sad version of myself, but I had to learn. I had to understand how *this was the new normal*, the present way I had to live, the short path on hospital linoleum I had to stumble through until I learned to walk again. I was no longer the non-tenure track professor who scurried from class-to-class on the busy days; I was no longer the non-tenure track professor on three different committees who read student essays about wanting to travel, wanting to *test out of* basic English, wanting to get published on our student site. I was no longer the roller derby blocker who could get lower on the track than anyone else, so low my ass was almost touching the floor, dammit, so quick to dig my skates into the rink and halt like a hockey player that I could turn and make it twenty feet behind the pack of skaters before anyone else could stop. I was no longer the baton twirler who—although years ago and really not something I thought about much at all—won the solo category at nationals because my front neck rolls were better than anyone else's, and my technique and speed rivaled the best in the world. I was no longer the person who picked up my phone in the middle of the night to counsel a friend through an alcohol-steeped mental breakdown over a lover breaking up with them and not wanting them back.

I was now a brain cancer patient in a hospital-sponsored hotel room who was attempting to match her shoulders to one another in a sad attempt to dance to a song no one else could hear. I was now a person who wore a foot-up brace and an air cast and struggled to get into Ubers and then had to answer questions about *how I sprained my ankle* when I actually did not sprain my ankle at all. I was now a person who listened to Tanya Tucker's "Delta Dawn" while having my brain microwaved by gamma rays. I was now a person who pretended to shop for vacations at Target when I was actually spending money to make myself feel pretty because brain cancer makes me feel like a naked rat, exposed to these doctors and nurses and research teams who want to cure me but actually have no idea if this is even possible. I was now a person who swallowed four blank white chemo pills every morning in an attempt to shrink and destroy any cancer cells that might have hung out in my brain after surgery.

I forgot I had Whitney Houston's "I Wanna Dance with Somebody (Who Loves Me)" on my playlist.

I must be cautious that I do not fall or hurt myself in this hotel room. There are no emergency pulls or strings to call a nurse if I stumble or trip or lose control of my right side.

(Who Loves Me)? No one, not really.

I am Dancing on My Own, which is a Robyn song, but just as good as Whitney.

Fight me.

I do not work as well as I once did, and I do not know if I will work again.

But I try. I watch myself in the mirror, no matter how awkward I feel, and realize I still have a sense of rhythm, a sense of myself. I have always known who I am. No matter the shitty people I have dated, the writing rejections, the times I sat on the derby bench and didn't play because I was not good enough to face the competitors or impress my coaches, the instances where I dropped my baton when I shouldn't have because I was thinking about the next trick or the fucking shiny stick just slipped through my hand, I have never forgotten how strong I am, how I smile with genuine kindness to strangers, how I have the desire to love every stray, cold cat who does not have a home.

I have always been slightly asymmetric.

My haircut.

My personality.

My writing.

Now, my shoulders. My arms. My hips.

My dancing, on my own, in a hospital-sponsored hotel room, too early at night to be cool or fun or acceptable for anyone else but me.

the hawthorne hotel, the dash

I watch old *Twilight Zone* episodes in my hotel room. There is one where this guy believes he is in heaven; his guide will give him anything he wants, including money, women, gambling wins, and the finest food. He becomes bored, though. He realizes his wins are more charity than luck, and he simply wants nothing more to do with heaven.

His guide laughs. This fucker is in hell, but he has no idea.

I consider the similarities.

I am in a nice hotel. I am ordering room service and watching whatever I want on television. I am buying shit at Target I do not need.

But this is hell, or a lot like hell, I imagine.

I only have these things because I am in a shit show of a life where I have lost control of the things I love.

Perhaps I should have learned we can never control what we love.

Control is the opposite, the opposite of heaven, the opposite of learning to care without demands.

Control spreads faster than brain cancer, faster than leg seizures that move, shake, and wiggle me into the next phase of my life that does not seem possible, does not seem real, not at all.

the hawthorne hotel, the dash/old salem, the dash

The chemo makes me feel sick makes me feel sick makes me feel sick.

I leave the nausea medication at home in Boone because I do not know for sure if I will be staying the weekend in Winston-Salem. As someone who has endured type one diabetes for 31 years, I know better than to leave medication at home, ever; still, the nausea cure was with my original chemo medication that I might have taken but ended up abandoning because of my admittance into the clinical trial. So, that nausea medication was with the other medication that got left behind at home, and here I am at a hotel in Winston-Salem with a lot of nausea and no medication and the hope I can continue writing this book before I die.

I finally feel sick I finally feel sick I finally feel sick.

What if you actually don't have brain cancer, my sister says on the phone. She's a conspiracy theorist and believes my doctors may have given me a *false positive MRI* to make me pay for brain surgery and for *them to fill my body with poison.*

I tell my darkest secrets to complete strangers.

No one expects the answer I give, so they always ask.

What happened to your leg? Sprained ankle? Take a fall?

This depends on how I feel. Sometimes, I answer *yep, took a fall. Sprained it pretty badly. Should be better soon.*

Other times, I answer *I have brain cancer.*

I tell the tour guide at the Old Salem Visitor's Center this. She works at the upstairs exhibit of Southern Folk Arts, and no one else has visited her exhibit today except for me. It is early yet, so her guidance still has energy. She moved from the Midwest to North Carolina, but she does not tell me why; she does tell me that she maintains a keen interest in Southern arts. I take an extended look at a fanciful chest made by someone in West Virginia in the 1800s. After studying the British Victorians for so long, I wonder why I rarely cared about Americans during this time. As it turns out, they were woodworking in my home state while the British were writing really long novels and making one another wear corsets.

My sister lost her battle with cancer, the guide tells me. *But she had a different outlook than you. She was fearful.*

One weird thing about this cancer ordeal is that people assume they know me. Friends. Strangers. Doctors. *You're so positive*, they say as they pat me on the back. *You're going to be just fine.* Is it my smile? I smile a lot. I always have. I even felt guilty when women started the initiative to stop smiling when men told them to; although I supported this mission fully, I also knew I could never stop showing my teeth to everyone I encountered. *This was just me.* I can never help myself.

Brain cancer diagnosis?

Smile.

You're having a craniotomy today.

Smile.

The hospital's pot roast looks like dog food.

Smile.

But this does not translate to happiness. My face can do whatever the fuck it wants; this does not mean my mind, my body, my soul agree with my perfectly aligned teeth. I am not fake—I am complicated.

Very complicated.

Well, I try to stay positive, I say. *It's not always easy. I have a hard time somedays.*

I cannot help but stare at the portrait of a young, blonde 18th century American boy. His painting hangs above a wooden chest made by someone from the South Carolina low country. He points to something outside of the painting, but he keeps his blue eyes focused on his artist. He knows exactly what he is doing: creeping out museum patrons over 100 years later.

His gaze scares me more than my cancer.

He points to a secret room, where I peek through the door.

Now that's for a special tour where patrons pay for an extra ticket, my guide tells me. *We do not keep anything in that room protected, so we have to watch people very closely.*

Tell me about that book in there, I say.

No one ever asks about the book, she says as she pulls up the info on her iPad. She shows me a reproduction of the book, but her inability to stop swiping through the iPad version of the text reveals her nervousness. No one has asked her about the book, so she has no monologue prepared. *I don't know much about it, let's see here, it looks old, really old…I do know that someone found it on their back porch. Didn't know what they had. Really just had no idea.*

I thank her for the information.

Now, if you want to have lunch, there's a tavern. I don't know if you're on any special diet…

I'm on the eat whatever the fuck I want diet.

I eat pretty much whatever, I say. *I love sugar.*

Now, by the time my sister was at the end, she didn't eat any sugar at all.

I'm in the beginning, I say. *The very beginning.*

The very beginning can seem so close to the very end, I want to say, but instead I just smile.

This is what I do.

the hawthorne hotel, the dash

I don't tell my new Tinder matches I have brain cancer, but I do casually respond to a couple new messages.

I am bored.

That info is in my profile, but I don't think anyone reads those things.

Instead, I just listen to them talk about their work days. What they see out the window. What kind of treats their dogs ate that day.

I don't tell them I never plan to meet them because I will most likely be dead.

It's nothing personal, I could say, but small talk has its place.

boone, north carolina

SZ, 36, died from aggressive brain cancer. (As an aside, she would like everyone to know she hated obituaries that refuse to say how the person died. Perhaps this was just a minor pet peeve, but without writing the cause of death, most readers assume suicide or a car wreck when a young person dies. And sure, her death was a suicide of sorts—it was a car wreck of sorts. Her own brain killed her; her own brain switched gears suddenly and crashed her body car off the cliff. Still, she had nothing to do with this. She was not driving. SZ also knew most obituaries charge by the word, so this aside is strictly for free social media posts and not for any printed obituary.) Type one diabetes, which SZ had for 31 years, probably also had some relation to her death, but it's easier to blame brain cancer. It was more prevalent at the end and quickly stagnated her life and murdered her in a slow parade of seizures, rehabilitation, chemotherapy, and radiation.

Before all of this madness occurred, SZ received a Ph.D. from Auburn University and taught Rhetoric and Composition at Appalachian State University in Boone, North Carolina. She played roller derby with Appalachian Roller Derby. She finds it odd how similar writing an obituary is to composing a literary journal bio. She loved writing flash fiction and found much success in the genre months before her death.

SZ, known as Hammer to most of her friends, left behind a lot of motherfuckers. (Again, that word will not be in the actual obituary, but it feels appropriate enough for this book.) She is survived by her parents, Ted and Jenifer; one sister, Sarah.; her first cousins Emily (Loren Pilcher), Kyle (Kelly Binderim), Megan (Joey Ihavenoideawhatthefuckhislastnameis), and Cathleen; her aunt Tamara; her mom's brother Jeff, his wife Jennin, and their children: Javy and Miranda (twins), Julian and Ava (more twins), and Joscylin; her friends, Nodya Boyko (David Roisen), Jenna Cucco Ross (Derek Ross), Lauren Feeney, JC (Miriam), Shaina Crump, Lindsay Darnell, Emily Wentworth, Amanda Morris, Michaela Keleman, travis michael (please keep this in lowercase), Amy Lilly, Betsy Riggs, Vanessa George, Jodi Rowe, and Jessica Blevins. She is also survived by her beloved friends and colleagues at Appalachian State: Mel Wahab, Hailie Bryant, Gail York, and Kate Birgel.

Chris.

Alex.

(More on Alex later.)

Most importantly, SZ is survived by her pets, who were her heart: Prufrock (cat), Duffles (cat), and Gatsby (dog).

SZ was preceded in death by her paternal grandparents: Velva and Lawrence S.; her maternal grandparents: Doris Jo and Bill Childers; her maternal great grandmother: Edna Reeves; her paternal aunt, Lois Robison; her paternal uncle, Roger.; and, her cousin, James.

Her dad had a very big family; there are more, but those were the ones she felt closest to.

In her death, she would like people to realize the following: type one diabetes is an autoimmune disease not caused by lifestyle. She would also like for people to never vote for a moron like Donald Trump ever again and realize that people are different and have needs and desires that no one should attempt to control or fear. SZ, in her death, would wish for people to be kind, sarcastic, and any acceptable combination of the two. She thinks people should read more and pay more attention to the way they write. Yes, this also refers to text messages.

She would like to note that her romantic partners throughout her life should have never accused her of being *insane* or *crazy* when they were the ones who treated her like trash and expected her to take it all in and do nothing about it. Seriously? They put her through some bullshit and then just wanted her to walk away as if it never happened.

Please.

Get control of yourselves.

Overall, SZ had a pretty decent life. This was due to cats, a lot of worthless Lifetime movies, and writing flash fiction about what ailed her.

She thought people should stop being sad about stupid shit when their friend or loved one might be dealing with the end of their life. (And yes, this is personal. Very personal.) She was also a really good baton twirler and thinks people should consider baton twirling a serious sport. Twirling and roller derby gave her confidence and allowed her to feel powerful and strong. SZ regrets not seeing all the memes from 2019 forward, the second season of *Friends from College* (although she and her sister are likely the only two people excited about the release), and any other weird Darren Aronofsky movies following *mother!*. She regrets not beating Candy Crush, though she did get very far. She would like to leave this world with the message that roller derby is changing the world, and people should pay attention.

the hawthorne hotel, the dash.
I'm sorry you're sad, I message JC.
  How did you know? she asks.
  Sometimes I can just tell.

wake forest baptist hospital, comprehensive cancer center, the dash
The volunteer guarding the Cancer Center snacks believes I do not belong.

I ask for some orange juice as I wait for my doctor to deliver unprecedented news regarding my clinical trial.

My blood sugar drops, and I need some goddamn juice.

I suppose we might have some, she says as she glares at my green toboggan and bright orange tennis shoes. *Let me check the fridge.*

I do not feel sick I do not feel sick I do not feel sick.

I am certain she thinks I am waiting with someone, waiting for someone, and just got hungry. I'm sure she thinks I am just thirsty and just wanting to be a pain in the ass.

I have a low blood sugar, I say.

I think this may help.

It does not.

Everyone is mad at me.

She hands me the six-ounce can of orange juice with regret. How dare I steal this juice from old people with cancer! How dare I request a can of juice when there are people here who might need it? Who do I think I am to make these types of demands?

I am good at hiding.

No one understands I am about to die.

I look normal.

I have not lost my hair yet.

The only indication: the air cast on my leg that helps me keep my stability.

No one can tell I have brain cancer and will likely be dead within a year.

comprehensive cancer center, office visit, the dash

Patient one in clinical trial BAL101553 is almost gone.

These are not the exact words Dr. Stroupe uses, of course.

He says *the first patient is in the hospital. He's weeks ahead of you in the trial…and we've…well, we've determined that his ailments are from the drug interaction. Likely not the cancer itself.*

My doctor and my two research nurses, Punchy and Amy, watch my reaction. I have started putting my hands in my jacket pockets so I do not fidget while medical professionals speak to me.

You have two options. Some people want to continue with the clinical trial no matter what. They have committed; they are in. Others hear this kind of information and want out, immediately.

I need to know more, I say. *What kind of symptoms did the other patient have?*

I know the doctor cannot tell me the other patient's name or identifying information, but I do not want to call him Patient One. I am not certain how *the Other Patient* differs greatly from *Patient One*, but I need to make the distinction.

Well…it's not good.

A heart attack? Some sort of blood disorder? A stroke?

He might turn the corner, Amy says.

The corner from what?

He just might, Punchy says.

He's weeks ahead of you, the doctor says.

I know what this means; they are trying to get me to leave the trial. I am compliant. I do not want to be in the hospital, not in this way. This is not: come to the hospital for radiation and a couple appointments, which is bad enough. This is: *oh my fucking god he's almost dead* type of *in the hospital.*

It's up to you, my doctor says. *Totally up to you. If you want out of the trial, we will flush that chemo out of your system and put you on Temodar, which you received but never started. Do you still have it?*

I do.

I cannot remember if it's in my fridge or my pantry or in my makeup bag. The Temodar, the chemo, is somewhere. Just hanging out.

Waiting. Watching. Hoping.

I…I don't think I want to do the trial, I say.

Everyone breathes.

We will take a couple days to get the BAL out of your system, and then we will proceed with the Temodar. You can start the Temodar on Thursday.

Two vacation days.

Dr. Stroupe leaves the room. One of his kids, I have heard, has the flu. I am sure he is busy, worried about *the Other Patient*, and concerned for his children. But, he stopped by to tell me to stop taking the drug, to stop poisoning my body with some drug that would try to kill me like *the Other Patient.*

I appreciate my doctor.

I have this moment of panic, this moment of fright, for *the Other Patient.* I am sure, I am certain, he thought the drug gave him more hope for *beating this,* for *killing this fucking brain cancer.* And now here he was, dying in the hospital from the clinical trial drug that was supposed to save us all.

We've determined that his ailments are from the drug interaction.

He might turn the corner.

I want fucking out of here.

The doctor leaves the room after shaking my hand. Dr. Stroupe is warm, caring.

His children have the flu.

Do you have any questions for us? Amy asks me. She gives me that look, the look letting me know I can ask them anything I want.

But I don't.

I am too frightened to ask anything more.

We are really, really glad you decided to drop out of the trial, Amy says. Punchy shakes her head to agree.

This must have been bad. Really, really bad.

Once we get you back on Temodar, you can complete the cycle and get pretty much the full dosage.

After this failed clinical trial, I still have hope, although hope is a word that has lost its meaning.

We know what Temodar does.

We know what to expect.

We know that it might get rid of your brain cancer for a minute, but then the cancer will return, they should have said.

I knew what they meant.

We know what Temodar does.

We know.

We are just so glad you aren't part of the trial anymore. Now you don't have to do the ultrasound IV we were going to set you up with, Punchy says.

I smile. It is genuine. It is for the first time today.

the road between boone and the dash

My sister forgets her driving hat, so the day goes to shit.

Perhaps she has spent too much time in New York City; perhaps she has spent too much time watching cab and Uber drivers truncate long sentences of traffic into a few sharp words that everyone has learned to mute.

We stop so she can throw up.

Things that may have made my sister sick:

1. Her period.
2. The two beers she drank last night, though unlikely.
3. The nacho fries from Taco Bell that she left out for half the day and decided to eat on her way to pick me up.
4. The altitude.
5. The curvy roads.
6. Most likely the nacho fries.
7. She forgot her driving hat.

We stop twice on the way home so she can vomit. *The irony!* she yells from outside the car. I am too tired, too frustrated to understand if this is actually irony or not. Irony. It became one of those things that people talked about so much, all definitions lost their meaning. Regular irony. Dramatic irony.

The opposite of what was intended.

But what was intended? I was supposed to vomit. But now maybe the BAL101553 drug will do worse things to my body. *You have time to flush it out of your system*, the doctor assured me.

But did I?

We do not forget the driving hat the next morning. Sarah is smiling, the sun is rising, and she's playing Skrillex on her Pandora.

I don't give a fuck what people say about Skrillex, she says. *He's cool as fuck.*

I do not feel sick I do not feel sick I do not feel sick.

And then Sarah is sick again, somehow.

She vomits up everything. I hear her. I hold my own stomach so I do not echo in response. Sarah sounds as if she drank two gallons of water last night. Skrillex still blares from the car's Bluetooth; I do not recognize the song. I know nothing about cool music, past or present.

She returns to the car and clicks her seatbelt. Sarah pulls a toboggan over her blonde and lime green hair. The lime green section resembles the sherbet I ate with my left hand in the hospital.

I have a new driving hat now, she says as we head toward the hospital. The sunset hurries ahead of us, and we know we can take our time.

boone, north carolina

Night brings thoughts of death.

I don't know if it's the darkness, the disease, or the despair.

A combination.

I focus on the feeling of death. Not death itself but the actual physical sensation of dying. My friends warn against this. *You can't know until it happens*, they say. *You're not going to die. You can't. You can't leave us*, they say. *You're going to beat this*.

But I am tired, and I need to prepare.

I have always favored preparation over spontaneity. However, my best teaching days went unplanned.

Will everything just go black? I do not know if I will want morphine. I say that now; I also said I didn't want weed during chemo, but then I did want it, and yes, it does help the nausea immensely. Will I experience a burst of fireworks in my brain that will burn me from the inside out? This could happen during radiation, perhaps, but I do not know if the tumor will just continue to spread or if it will self-destruct in a kamikaze mission. I mean, the tumor is gone, but I saw the notes: none of the doctors are certain if the tumor has already started to grow again or if the whiteness on the screen is just the swelling.

The swelling that still prevents me from moving my foot.

Will the seizures continue? Will I still take the medication that prevents seizures? I want to know these things but I don't. I search but refuse to read the articles. I'm lost in a mass of information that becomes a tumor of its own; the more the information grows, the less I know, the more I am afraid.

I do not want to shut my eyes.

The surrounding darkness is enough; the blackness of the back of my eyelids seems too much to bear so I stare at a string of dust on the ceiling and wonder how I can fall asleep, how I can awake the next morning, how I can prepare myself for another day.

boone, north carolina

I dream of JC.

Not her, specifically, but what she does for me.

In the dream, I walk to downtown Boone. I have no pain or discomfort in my leg. The snow is pure and pale, unlike the dirty white mess that befell my apartment the night before. My mind does not know where I am headed, but my legs continue to walk in a specific direction.

I arrive at a log cabin tucked between two storefronts. No one can see the cabin, but I know it is there. I can see it, and I know how to enter. There is a slight incline to reach the cabin, but I am able to handle the steep, powdery challenge.

I am not cold, but I should be.

Everyone bustles around me, past the storefronts, into the stores. The people wear muted scarves and gloves. This was what Christmas looked like, I tell myself. I was not around—I was having and recovering from brain surgery.

I am not cold, but I should be.

I open the door to the cabin. I do this without a key; JC has been expecting me.

She stands in the middle of the cabin's main room. Like a secret, she holds the cabin's key between both hands. It is a slightly rusted skeleton key. This is not necessarily an important detail, but I have never seen a house that actually uses a skeleton key.

And please don't forget: I really like keys.

JC wears burgundy gloves to keep the secret close and hidden. We make eye contact, and she hands me the key.

Whenever I see her, JC's eyes are a different color. Each time. Today they are green. Christmas tree green. The *human mood ring*.

This place has healed me from my sadness, she says. *And now the house will heal you from your sickness.*

The Healing House.

There are books scattered everywhere. A stoked fire. Warm blankets. The books have weathered covers. They are ancient and old but not tired. They are full of words and life.

Stay as long as you like, she says. *You won't need me but bring me the key when you are done. You might want to stay forever. You can if you would like. No one will question you.*

I am warm, and I should be. I am comfortable without thought, just as I was before brain cancer. I have no nausea or sickness. I do not miss anyone or feel the need for company.

JC pulls her gray sweater tightly around her waist. I don't know why JC typically wears a belt. She smiles as she leaves and tells me nothing more about the cabin. I know this is a secret, though. I know no one else can see the house; no one else knows I am here. No one will try to find me, and I am pleased with this.

Once she is gone, I make myself comfortable on the couch. I know there must be a cat around somewhere; this would not be my cabin, my comfortable space, without a cat. I rummage through the fridge and cabinets until I find the ingredients to make hot chocolate.

I never drank hot chocolate until I saw it on the hospital menu in December. They made me order the sugar-free version, but it still tasted better than water, better than ice. Now I want it all the time.

I do not give insulin coverage for the hot chocolate, so I know this must be more than a Healing House. This is where I will come when I die, when I am done. I do not know if I really believe in heaven, but this will be a place I can rest, a place where I can find peace. My leg works here, and I do not experience any type of nausea or discomfort.

Stay as long as you would like, JC says.

I am surprised when I wake up the next morning in my regular bed, my right leg weakened by a full night's sleep, and my throat full of vomit and exhaustion.

wake forest baptist hospital, comprehensive cancer center, the dash

On the eighth day of radiation, I finally see a woman around my age in the changing room. Before radiation, patients must put on these blue-and-white pin-striped gowns so we can be spotted by the technicians. That's not the real reason, of course, but I tell myself that because it's funny. Because I need to make myself laugh. Because I need a reason.

The woman and I exchange looks of recognition. *Fuck, dude. How did this happen?* the glances say. *We're fucked, ya know? Totally fucked. We are too young for this, too fresh. How did this happen, you know?*

After my treatment finishes, I lock myself in the bathroom to put on makeup. I have no reason to do this, but I want to look like myself. My old self. When I unlock the bathroom, I see my new friend putting on makeup in front of the changing room mirror. We do not smile, but we stare at one another's mascara.

You look good, I think. You look good.

boone, north carolina

My sister and I have always had this joke.

Sarah, I have something to tell you.

She knows what happens next, but she plays along.

Yes?

I'm dying.

And then I stare into the corner of the room or the sky and attempt to maintain serious composure.

Whoever laughs first loses.

nowhere

The funny thing about cancer is that it doesn't make you sick; the medicine does. The cure makes you very very very fucking sick.

boone, north carolina

Some friends are mad at me.

You're shutting us out.

Maybe I am.

I haven't really thought about this much—I have been preoccupied. However, I've told my story to strangers. To Uber drivers. To people in restaurants who want to know how I *sprained my ankle*. To my vet receptionist who asked why I had to have an afternoon appointment.

I'm getting cancer treatments in Winston-Salem, I say.

These things seem easier to say to strangers. The words emerge from my mouth before I can even think about them. With friends, I have to think. I have to choose my words. I have to attempt to avoid upsetting anyone. With strangers, I can say whatever I wish. I can say *I have brain cancer* without worrying about the weight of anyone else's feelings. I will never see most of these strangers again, and if I do, well, they will know I am still alive.

The young woman with brain cancer is still alive.

boone, north carolina

A sample of messages I receive from people I have not spoken to in quite some time:

In sixth grade, I snapped your bra strap. I thought it was funny. I am really sorry. I should have never done that. Especially with the #metoo movement, I feel terrible for what I did.

I have no memory of anyone snapping my bra strap, but I commend the dude who sent the message for owning up to this.

Good for him.

I am really sorry to hear about your prosthetic leg. I can't imagine what it must be like to deal with the loss of your limb along with the cancer diagnosis.

I do not have a prosthetic leg.

My sister and I speak about *the prosthetic leg message* whenever things get quiet.

We laugh.

How long did it take you to put on your prosthetic leg this morning?

Damn, like three hours. I hate this thing.

We laugh we laugh we laugh.

I know you don't know me that well, but…

Those messages break me. People who *don't know me that well* take the time to message me or send me a card to let me know they care. They think of me. They wonder how I feel or what I do to pass the time.

I haven't talked to you in a long time, but…

…but these messages mean something. I am too tired to respond to most of them, but they mean something, anything, everything.

wake forest baptist hospital, comprehensive cancer center, the dash

Before my diagnosis, I pictured chemo taking place in a room with other patients. These patients would all be hooked up to IVs and maybe reading, maybe talking to one another, maybe sleeping. Occasionally, someone would puke into an airplane bag, and machines would whir and beep to let nurses know everyone was still alive.

I did not picture taking pills by myself and logging those pills onto a chart so my nurses could keep track of the time, amount, and side effects. This log was only for the study drug, the failed BA101553, but still, not something I imagined. I did not know chemo was even offered in pill form and that yes, most brain cancer patients take chemo orally. I did not imagine keeping those study pills in the fridge of a hotel room and writing myself a note—CHEMO IN FRIDGE—so I would not forget to take the drugs first thing in the morning, as soon as I woke up.

I did not imagine any of this.

Before my diagnosis, I pictured radiation taking place in a room resembling an MRI space; I was close. I did not imagine getting to know other patients because everyone has radiation at the same time each day.

I did not think that the sister of the lady who has radiation in room one before me would teach me about the bell.

Whenever someone finishes their radiation treatment, they ring a bell. The first time this happens, I am sitting in an ergonomic chair, almost asleep. I jump when I hear the ring. I had seen the bell before, but I thought it was symbolic. A donation of some sort, a prop to make the place look pretty.

That means they are done, the lady tells me as she claps. *Done with their treatments! Amazing.*

I want to be one of those people.

I want to ring the bell.

I did not know, I did not imagine any of this.

boone, north carolina

Eventually, people stop telling me I *look great*.

This was a common response for the first month.

I can't believe you just had brain surgery. You look amazing. I can't believe you have brain cancer. You look great!

Now.

How are you…doing? Are you…feeling okay? Are you…sick?

I kind of feel sick I kind of feel sick I kind of feel sick.

I have not thrown up, but nausea has become a sidekick. A constant friend. A reminder that my entire life has changed.

I start taking a marijuana tincture that helps the nausea subside, but I still wake up every three hours and feel uneasy. Unsteady. Unwell. My foot occasionally lifts itself toward the ceiling in a weird prayer, and I wonder if it is some sort of seizure, some sort of indication that the tumor has returned and I am fucked.

I am definitely fucked.

We can't tell, the doctor said the last time I had an MRI. *There's still too much swelling to know if the tumor has returned or if it's just fluid.*

I do not believe the tumor has returned, but I have been wrong about this before. I trusted my gut, trusted my intuition that the tumor was just a strange anomaly and not cancerous. I stayed positive (as everyone told me I must do), and I repeated over and over again *benign benign benign*. I thought if I did this, I would be right. I would be correct. I would be healthy. I would return to my parents' home in West Virginia, rest, and learn to walk again. I would persevere, everyone would be so proud of me, and I would show how just *thinking about the best* can actually make it happen.

And then that's not what happened, and everything went to shit.

Some friends find themselves frustrated with my *negativity, my depressed thought patterns.*

You just have to hope for the best and stay positive. That's been proven to help cancer.

But sometimes, there's just no positive thoughts to be found. I read statistics online. I search forums. I hear about how people with glioblastomas typically live *about a year* after the diagnosis. That treatment prolongs life but does not cure the cancer or prevent tumors from reoccurring.

You look great.

After I start the clinical trial chemo, I eat two, maybe just one meal per day. I have no appetite. I wake up in the middle of the night with hypoglycemia because I don't eat. I drink some juice and force some dry crackers into my mouth. I chew. I go through the motions. I attempt to eat the entire package but give half the crackers to my dog instead.

My sister sleeps on the futon but hears me rummage around for my nighttime snacks.

I know she worries.

We spend the late afternoons and weekends doing fun activities, sister things. We go shopping. We go to the pet store and search for outfits worthy of her tiny dog. We get Starbucks and take selfies. We play a modified version of charades from a phone app.

We watch *Wheel of Fortune* and *Jeopardy* before I fall asleep.

She was the first female Supreme Court Justice…

…Judge Judy! Sarah answers, and we both laugh.

You look great, Trebek tells me through the television. He had brain surgery around the same time as I did, but I think his was for a different reason. Blood clots. Goddammit, Trebek. I've always loved you, even though you're a total asshole.

You look great, Trebek. You look great.

boone, north carolina

I start talking to Alex more after surgery and my diagnosis.

Alex, JC's friend from Thanksgiving.

At Thanksgiving, we talked about Davenports—which are a specific type of sofa—and what we did for a living. Small talk about big things. Alex and I connected because she has hypoglycemia to such an extreme that she must check her blood sugar daily.

I am convinced Alex checks her blood sugar more than I do.

Before all this shit happened, I would send Alex pictures of empty cracker and fruit snack packages in my bed. This would happen after my blood sugar dropped in the middle of the night; I would get up, take snacks back to my bed, and after binging on the snacks, let my cold sweat marinate the plastic wraps. The caption would read *hypo last night?* with a string of laughing emojis. She always responded with something sweet, which made me feel good.

Validated. Strong, even. Worthy.

Don't forget: I dreamt about Alex.

In the dream, I cry about everything that happened.

Before this, I rarely allowed myself to cry at all. I also do not know Alex terribly well, so I do not know how she would actually respond to me crying about a craniotomy.

Boo fucking hoo.

But in the dream, Alex smiles and tells me *everything will be okay, I promise*.

For some reason, I believe her.

asheville, north carolina

Sarah is the worst driver ever.

(She snooped through my computer one night and read some of this book. She claims she read the line *Sarah is the worst driver ever* in the unedited, unreviewed text. I do not remember writing this, but perhaps I did. I need to search the text later to see if there is any truth to this. For now, I will write it again as a refrain, as a private joke, as a way to connect with my sister after I am gone.)

We go to Asheville on a Saturday when I do not have radiation or chemo. I am between chemo cycles; I am no longer in the clinical trial, but I have not yet started the old/new chemo that has been proven to work, kinda but not really.

Or something like that.

Sarah is the worst driver ever.

There are only backroads from Boone to Asheville. I know these roads well—I commuted through their snow-dusted hairpin turns and decades-old potholes for four years. Because of the two-hour length and dangerously icy elevation, people thought I was insane. I would leave school some evenings and drive home to Asheville without knowing if I was actually on the road or blurring through the white wilderness; sometimes, the snow was so pervasive I felt as if I was plowing through the Alaskan unknown instead of Western North Carolina.

Now I cannot remember which way to turn.

Sarah keeps asking, and I keep fucking up.

Everything looks both foreign and familiar.

When we arrive in Asheville, Sarah and I re-create the times we would hangout downtown when we both lived in the city. One semester, I had Mondays off, and so did she. Although we both lived in Asheville, we would hop around downtown like tourists and do indulgently fun shit no one else would ever do with us. There are certain things you can only do with a sister, and drinking coffee from a corner double-decker bus while listening to people go on and on about *the healing properties of activated charcoal masks* is one of them.

We drink our coffee and take stupid selfies and videos. Sarah draws hearts on the frosted windows and accidentally spits coffee on her lap.

When we leave, she takes a picture of me drawing a cat head on a giant outdoor chalkboard. We realize later that the chalkboard has BEFORE I DIE written across the top.

BEFORE I DIE I WILL DRAW A CAT FOR YOU.

That's kind of dark, she says, and we both laugh.

We go to the Fine Arts Theatre and watch *I, Tonya*. We drink root beer and marvel at Allison Janney's performance as Tonya Harding's mom. Although we were both young during Tonya's disastrous Lillehammer Olympics, we feel guilty for not supporting her more.

Fucking amazing athlete, I say.

That's life, I guess, Sarah says. *Even the good ones get fucked.*

I assume she's also talking about me, but neither one of us comment.

Although I am exhausted and barely make it down the stairs of the Fine Arts Theatre, we go to the French Broad Chocolate Lounge to meet our cousin Kyle and his wife, Kelly. Kyle, more of a brother than a cousin, presents me with a framed, cross-stitched masterpiece of 1-up mushrooms from Super Mario.

I made you some extra lives, he says as he gives me a hug.

There is fog instead of snow on the way home. Sarah can barely see and swerves off the road whenever she pulls out her phone or needs to scratch her eye.

Sarah is the worst driver ever.

I have never loved any human more.

boone, north carolina

Although my foot would not quit dropping and dragging behind me during my recovery from surgery and physical therapy, almost two months later, my right foot keeps pulling itself toward the ceiling like a possessed puppet.

Is there still swelling in my brain?

Is my tumor back?

Is my foot just fucking mad at me for all its been through?

I am also mad, foot, so please take a second and compose yourself.

I keep thinking of that weird rumor about me having a prosthetic leg.

I do not.

I have another seizure the next morning. My first one since surgery. I try to hold my right foot down with my left leg, but I am unsuccessful. My right foot and calf shiver in the coldness of fear. It's as if my marionette foot is made of instrument strings instead of invisible wire; my foot and leg quiver as if someone has plucked them and expected a song.

All I can offer is the unknown.

A few moments of silence.

The misery of a good time.

I decide not to tell anyone about this seizure. Nothing would change. I still have brain cancer. I still might have tumor regrowth. I still might have swelling in my head. I still have nausea.

I feel fucking sick I feel fucking sick I feel fucking sick.

boone, north carolina

I read weird things on the internet about brain cancer patients and death.

I cannot confirm the accuracy of any of them.

A week before death, the patient may discuss packing bags or a suitcase and taking a trip.

My mom bought me luggage when I was in the hospital. Maybe she knew. Maybe she read the same article. Maybe she just wanted me to have a container for all the shit I acquired from Amazon Prime while I was unable to walk and in a rehab center full of elderly men.

They will likely become incontinent.

Will I have a catheter? Rubber sheets? Diapers at 36? Who is going to clean this shit up? My friends and colleagues who have offered *to do anything!*

Likely not change my diaper.

I'm fucking screwed. I'm going to die while taking a piss on myself and thinking about packing my luggage for a trip to the darkness, the unexplored.

I just want to go to the Healing House. Read books. Drink hot chocolate. Never again give an insulin injection.

Directly before death, they may utter the same phrase over and over again, as if they are chanting.

I do not feel sick I do not feel sick I do not feel sick.

boone, north carolina

JC and I go see a movie on the Sunday before I restart chemo.

The *normal chemo*. The one brain cancer patients typically take. The one that did not almost kill someone in a clinical trial.

Nausea: pervasive, and I cannot figure out why.

Hopefully: just from radiation. My doctor did not mention this would happen, but I read that *brain cancer radiation often causes nausea more than other types of radiation.* Sure, this was from the internet, where all of us get every modicum of bad information, but it's from the American Cancer Society website, so I figure there is some truth to it?

I hope.

Perhaps: the tumor has already started growing again and is causing the nausea.

Also likely: the clinical trial chemo finally caught up to me and is responsible for making me feel ill.

I almost cancel on JC, but I go. Sarah decides to stay home to clean the apartment and have some time alone. JC seems disappointed, and part of me wonders if she has a crush on my sister. My sister resembles a more diminutive version of JC's ex-wife, and I cannot get that stray thought to leave my head.

I get to the movie theater early; JC arrives late.

She asks if she can give me a hug, and I have trouble standing, trouble meeting her.

We watch *The Shape of Water.*

I sink into my seat and awkwardly play with my hands. JC does the same. I do okay, I do fine, until the lead female in the film turns over her daily calendar and the quote reads *Life is just the shipwreck of our plans.*

I cry I cry I cry.

I try to stop, but I cannot. I do not make any sound or indication I am crying. It just happens, and I think I may have to leave so JC does not know. Instead, I just sit and stare at the cinematically gorgeous film and let the tears pool below my chin and onto my shapeless orange shirt. I do not wipe my face or sniffle.

I do not think JC knows.

When the film ends, JC gives me a dog outfit for Claire, my sister's small, senior pup. A tad too small for her dog, JC believes the outfit might fit Claire perfectly. It is a sweet gesture, and I suddenly realize the outfit sat on JC's lap throughout the entire film.

JC is really nice.

I wish I had more time to spend with her, more time to get to know her.

More time.

Instead, I think about the shipwreck and wonder how soon I might drown, how soon I might have to say goodbye.

nowhere

My brain surgery scar is nothing more than a small line of red skin now penetrated by radiation five days per week.

Your surgeon did a great job.

Everyone says this. I believe them. He did do *a great job*. The shitty thing, though, is no matter how great my surgeon did, the cancer remains aggressive and will probably return.

Actually, glioblastomas are so pervasive that they never really go away. They sprout. They hide. They create their own blood vessels and support systems while no one looks, while no one watches.

I try to *stay positive*, to do all the right things, to *eat healthy and all that shit*, but I know I have very few guarantees.

I imagine my red surgery scar as the danger line on a piece of paper. This seems the best metaphor for my life: a piece of paper. I have written as much as I can, done my best, but this life, this paper is impermanent. The surgeon ripped the page from my skull and stapled it back into the notebook. Still, anyone could rip out and toss the page away whenever.

I do not know when this might happen, but I know it will happen soon.

Inevitably.

Please don't shred me.

Please do not forget my words.

Please remember me.

things you should not say to terminally ill people

1. Didn't you ever want kids?
2. You look great.
3. No, really. You look great.
4. Anything I can do for ya?
5. You're going to beat this.
6. Seriously, though. YOU LOOK GREAT.
7. Let me bring you all kinds of food you said you didn't like because although you don't like tomatoes or okra or olives, these are the foods that will cure you. My grandmother also had diabetes and cancer, and these foods cured her. CURED HER OKAY? Plus, I want you to see how awesome of a cook I am.
8. You just need to be more positive. Positivity cures cancer. Probably cures type one diabetes, too. You're just too negative and need to stop thinking this way. Stop shutting people out.
9. You're going to beat this because you have to. You have to for me. K? Great.
10. How do you still look so good?
11. It's a good thing you never wanted kids.
12. (Let's not forget Chole)—What are you going to blame being a bitch on now that your tumor is gone?
13. There are other things, but I cannot remember them now. I do not know if this is because of chemo, tumor regrowth, or just the stress of it all.
14. No, but seriously, you look so good right now.

nowhere

I always thought I would want to know.

I always thought I would want to know the day I would die, the hour, the minute. *I would be able to make certain, to make sure I would have done everything by then. Who wouldn't want to know? You could come to terms with your own mortality while telling your loved ones your honest, loving feelings toward them.*

What I did not think about: how I might be given a timeline (by the internet, if not anyone else), and I would not be able to fulfill that timeline because the walking, well, it comes and goes. It has improved so much, and I have even taken off the foot and ankle braces, but still. It's not like I would be able to walk around Iceland for three hours and take Polaroids with my brain that I could later develop on my tongue to show friends and family the final enjoyable moments of my life.

What I did not think about: how some of my friends and family would not react in expected ways, and I would not be able to control their reactions or stop them from saying stupid, insensitive things or prevent them from crying and feeling badly when I stayed as calm as a cat with a dish of turkey, eating piece-by-piece what was happening to me and just hoping I never choked on a bone.

I always thought I would want to know.

Instead of having deep, meaningful conversations with family and friends, I crash in my bed while my sister vacuums. Sometimes I reply to Instagram messages about new types of cat litter or movie reviews I find invalid. When I do desire to speak about mortality, the messages stop or the *you're going to beat this anyway, so it doesn't matter* messages come in return. Why? Because coming to terms with my death at 36 reminds people of their own mortality. My *terminal brain cancer* reminds my friends and family that oh, fuck, this could also happen to me, and I do not think I want to be reminded of that. *I'll send you socks, I'll send you candy, but please, do not mention how you're dying.* Do not mention how depressed you feel about this or *how much it bums you out.* Please, do not talk about how chemo and radiation make you feel nauseous, or how you cannot eat during the day but instead wake up in the middle of the night with a blood sugar so low you can't decide if the lack of ability to walk is from the right-side paralysis or the lack of energy from hypoglycemia.

Can you not mention that?

It just kinda bums me out.

Let's talk about the good times, you know. How we went to that roller derby bout in Asheville, and you shoulder popped that girl two feet taller than you, and when she fell, the arena's polished concrete bore an imprint of her trashy tattoo.

You're not going to die. If you die from this weird, rare, unexpected disease, then so could I. And I deserve more than that. I deserve to fall in love, to cry about my exes who have forgotten me, to spend my free time scrolling through dating apps and shopping for someone new and exciting. I deserve to keep working this *cool fucking job* I love, and I deserve to walk around eclectic bookstores in Asheville late at night with the deliciously bracing mountain air pervading my skin as I pick up local poetry books. I deserve to eat spicy chicken nuggets from Wendy's (when they return again, because they will) and dip them in sweet-and-sour sauce that has been waiting in this little package for me for days, weeks, months. Because I am a human and this is what I deserve.

People learn to sympathize with the dead; this is easy. You miss the dead. You wonder what they might have become, what conversations you might have had, what you might have created together between the two of you. You remember how you casually talked about a favorite band, a favorite book, Donald Trump's covfefe Tweet, snapshots of times you shared, and the instance you held their hand when they feared those final moments when no one knew what to expect.

People do not know how to sympathize with the dying. This is messier, stranger. It becomes easier to utter clichés and make food they won't eat instead of saying what you feel or what you think.

You're going to beat this.

You're going to beat this for me.

You're going to be okay, I know it.

You're too young and healthy.

YOU LOOK GREAT THOUGH.

If you don't beat this, then maybe I couldn't either.

No, you don't understand, you have to beat this because you represent strength and honesty and empowerment, and if you fail? Well then we all do.

Often, I have found myself the only one not upset, the only one not expressing discomfort.

Sympathizing with the dying translates to searching for something inside yourself you do not want to find. It's as disorganized as my silly string, monkey bread tumor. The lines are not defined, and no one knows what to do or say next.

I have complaints, but I do not necessarily have suggestions. I cannot control peoples' reactions or behaviors; they are doing the best they can, although they will not believe this.

Sympathy with the dying: let's send them more socks.

I have stopped responding to texts asking how I am doing.

I do not know how to respond or why I should.

How the fuck do you think I am doing?

Strangely, I have not minded the people who have disappeared, the people I haven't heard from at all.

I always thought I would want to know.

I do not.

I do not want to know.

wake forest baptist hospital, comprehensive cancer center, the dash
Session nine.

Fuck.

This is only my ninth session. I am not even a third of the way through radiation treatments, and I feel like I've been doing this for months instead of days.

I am now able to predict what happens next.

I know when the table will move, when the paparazzi cameras will flash.

(That's what I tell myself, anyway. I'm on a goddamn red carpet, and I'm famous. I never wanted to be famous, never a goal of mine, but it's better than knowing I am receiving radiation for brain cancer. Better than knowing my brain is in the microwave of medicine, cooking away.)

I don't know what the flashes actually mean, but that's when I smell skin burning and when the treatment is almost complete for the day.

I love and hate that scent.

nowhere

The worst: spending the last months of my life pleasing everyone else, doing what others expect of me, meeting their demands, making them happy.

boone, north carolina

Like an old lady, I organize my pills into a weekly planner. Occupational therapy had me practice this skill.

Planning: one of my neurocognitive deficits.

I do not feel deficit, but the doctors and therapists have made their decisions. Have given their prescriptions. Have decided what I have and what I do not.

Control: what I have always wanted and somehow failed to have.

A lifetime of type one diabetes has taught me how to manage medicine. Forget to take your insulin? You get really sick. Then you die.

This medicine is different.

Taking this medicine will make me really awful as it attempts to prolong my life.

The dying remains common, I suppose.

I do not feel sick I do not feel sick I do not feel sick.

boone, north carolina

My foot continues to move on its own. Without me giving it any commands. Is it waking up? Is this normal?

I remind myself to ask Jon, my neurologist and friend from graduate school.

I probably won't ask Jon. Or anyone else.

I have brain cancer. The last MRI showed I still have swelling. My brain, the balloon. I wish it would swell forever and lift me out of here.

The tumor could be back.

If it is, then nothing will be done. I have decided to forego any other surgeries, which I'm sure everyone will be pissed at me about. It's too traumatic, too much. I will not learn to walk again.

Learning to walk twice in a lifetime is enough.

I will not spend another month in a hospital with lovely nurses I do not know teaching me how to insert tampons with my left hand and wiping my ass when I have to take a shit.

I will not.

These are things you are supposed to worry about when you are old, when you are in a nursing home, when you've lived an entire Pangaea of hopes, regrets, and mistakes. These are not things you should worry about in your mid-30s. I was supposed to be meeting people, going on awkward dates, drinking wine with friends (or by myself) on Wednesday nights. I was supposed to be teaching my courses, helping freshmen students, hiding during my office hours while chugging cold coffee and spilling the last third of it on my already-sticky floor. I was supposed to be visiting my sister in NYC—not the other way around—and we were supposed to be bar hopping and visiting the Statue of Liberty with snow decorating her ankles.

I was supposed to spend Christmas with my family. I still have the handmade birdhouse I purchased for my dad. I bought the birdhouse from a guy at the mall who set up a kiosk by the doors. Birdhouse Guy could not believe I was *done with my Christmas shopping*, and it was not even Thanksgiving yet.

Everything was packed in the car, ready to go to my parents' house for Christmas. Everything was prepared. Everything was done early. Everything was ready.

Now when Sarah drives me to The Dash for radiation, we see the new growth of young Christmas trees dotting the roadsides like pointillism artwork. They need another year to become fully evergreen and prepared for a middle-class window display of slight extravagance and the appearance that *everything is just fine here, okay?*

They are not ready.

I was not ready.

boone, north carolina

JC tells me how her class is studying moral sentiment, specifically Adam Smith's *The Theory of Moral Sentiments.*

We talked a lot about death today. My students were discussing how we tend to feel sympathy for the dead, but this often doesn't help. The dead can't discern that we have sympathy for them, so why do we? What good does this do? Three people cried.

Were you one of them?

No, but I had feelings.

I don't respond for hours. I find the message somewhat insensitive but intriguing.

I am also jealous.

I am jealous I do not have a class to talk to about moral sentiments, the rising suicide rate on campus, or some stupid cat meme that appeared on the internet last night. I am jealous I do not wake up to an annoying alarm reminding me I *have young minds to teach about writing today.* I am even jealous of that anxious *oh my god I have to know what I'm talking about in front of these students today, or they are totally going to call me out on it* feeling that occurs roughly two seconds before any class begins.

I am jealous that instead of discussing how writers connect with the dead and how that represents a feeling we have all had or will have at some point, I am trapped in a hardened radiation mesh mask that makes me look like a serial killer. Until the table moves, I can see a reflection of myself during radiation.

I have always had a strong sense of who I am and what I want. Now, I just look like a derelict psychopath trapped in a cage by people who want to microwave my brain.

They are helping you, I remind myself. They are helping you.

JC notices my lack of response and sends a picture of an orange kitten licking its paw. I respond back with a meme of a dog wearing a cape.

Some things remain too difficult to discuss, too difficult to imagine.

wake forest baptist hospital, office visit, the dash

I have my follow-up with Jon, my friend from graduate school and now my neurologist, on a Wednesday afternoon, hours after my tenth radiation treatment.

I pass the time before the appointment by listening to a lady name Rose pound some tunes on the electric piano on the second floor of the Cancer Center. She asks if I have a favorite, and I say I do not. If I do have a favorite, which I'm not certain if I do or not, it would be some obscure mountain music song played by my father on the banjo.

Rose plays "The Rainbow Connection" before effortlessly sliding into "What a Friend We Have in Jesus." She turns to me mid-note and says *I have to play some religious tunes because we are sitting beside the meditation room.*

Fair enough, Rose. Fair enough.

I am nervous before meeting with Jon.

This does not feel like an appointment; it feels like coffee with a friend, minus the coffee and in a much more antiseptic setting where one of us is wearing a white coat.

Jon holds a manila folder as he walks into the room.

Hey, SZ. The kids made you some Valentine's Day cards. They have...a lot of stamps on them. The youngest isn't the best at art quite yet.

It is Valentine's Day.

I had forgotten.

The cards Jon and Veronica's children made me are adorable. They used markers, googly eyes, construction paper, and of course, stamps. They both signed their names on their respective cards so I would know just who made what. This is important when you are small—you must ensure your work is attributed to you and only you.

I suppose this is as equally important to adults.

My heart melts into my aortic cavities, into my lungs with the sweetness.

Jon does the regular neurological checks: touch your nose, touch my finger, follow the light, lift your knees, don't let me push down on your elbows.

I pass the tests, at least I think I do.

So you're seeing Dr. Stroupe, Jon says. I cannot call him Dr. Lucas. Dr. Jon Lucas, Ph.D. This sounds so professional, so austere. *If what is happening to you was happening to me or Veronica, I would see Dr. Stroupe. He's the best at what he does. He will make certain you receive the care you deserve.*

He's been amazing, I say. *He really spends time with his patients and always answers any questions I have.*

We both know how these things work, he says. *It's the same in medicine as it is in academics. Those who publish a lot of scholarly work do not always spend adequate time helping their patients. But Dr. Stroupe does both. He's known very well in his field, but he is always willing to hear what his patients say and answer any questions they have.*

And then nothing.

I did not expect this silence.

But now, because of this silence, because of this quiet, I know what is coming, what is about to happen.

I know this is when the serious shit is about to go down.

How…how are you doing?

I am doing okay, I say, *I…I'm 36. I'm so sorry. I didn't mean—*

—you don't have to be sorry, SZ. It's okay to cry about this.

I look at Jon and his eyes are red. Doctor. Friend. Father.

I just thought for sure it wasn't—cancer. I thought for sure, for certain.

I know, he says. *I know.*

But I guess I'm doing okay, you know? I try to still do the same stuff, the same things.

I do not know what I'm talking about anymore. I cry again. Jon's eyes are as red as the lettering on his resident white coat, and I know he is an empathetic doctor and will serve his patients well throughout the years.

You can cry, he says. *It's okay. You know, SZ, the older I get, the less I understand anything. Everything.*

I like that Jon does not tell me *I'm going to beat this* or *you're going to be fine.* He knows the statistics, the odds, the logos. He knows the risks and the likelihood I will not *beat this,* no matter how hard I try or how much of a positive attitude I maintain.

Are you writing? he asks.

Yes, I say. *It's the one thing that keeps me sane. It keeps me going.*

Good, he says as he leaves the room.

I hear him sniffling outside the door.

boone, north carolina

JC comes over so my sister can cut her hair.

I want to look like James Dean, JC says.

I collapse onto the futon so I can watch and feel involved in the experience. My sister works fast but with ultimate precision. Shards of JC's hair fall to my kitchen floor like silent glass. I'm surprised how dark JC's hair looks compared to the kitchen laminate; my mood ring human,

I think, although JC does not belong to me.

I am in my plaid nightgown. I do not care anymore who sees me or in what condition. I sat outside in the nightgown earlier. The weather was warm, and I wanted to hear the water below my apartment undulate and roll from the creeks and into the river.

Now I am sprawled on the futon with my legs spidered out behind me. No one will see anything, I think.

No one will ever see anything.

Sarah disappears to the bathroom to search for a clip, and JC talks to me about her class. She sits facing the dishwasher instead of me; Sarah said the lighting was better that way, and for some reason, JC does not turn around. As I stare at the back of her head, she talks to me about student interactions, class discussions, and the upcoming spring break. I am happy that JC's classes are going well, but I also feel a twinge of jealousy in my weak right leg. I feel everything there now. Every emotion, every hope, every negative thought.

I never lost feeling there.

I went to campus earlier to pick up a book from my office. I saw students leaving class—what would have been my class, my students, my time, my room—and I do not recognize any of them. I shouldn't recognize them, but I want to. I wish to know them, teach them, learn about them the way JC discusses how her own students were hugging and consoling one another after a tough class with discussions concerning gun control and race relations.

Who does your hair? JC asks me.

Sarah comes back into the kitchen with her missing clip. *Found it.*

A girl at Haircut 101 named Karrie, I say. *She only charges me six bucks. But she's studying to be a CNA. I'm not sure why anyone would want to do that, but I guess I don't have to worry. I'll be dead by the time she finishes her program.*

That's not funny, JC says as Sarah shapes her hair into a 1960s sex icon.

She says stuff like that all the time, Sarah says. *I guess if she thinks it's funny, it's okay to laugh.*

JC stares at the dishwasher. Her hair looks great, as if she went to a high-priced salon in New York City instead of a dying friend's kitchen.

boone, north carolina

Chris's girlfriend is moving to North Carolina.

She tells me this after asking if I *want updates.*

Umm…sure? I respond.

I don't know what to say. I'm not sure what the update concerns, and I've never known if I want information before I actually get it. I mean, did I want to know I had brain cancer? No, but I suppose I needed the information to move forward.

Rachel is moving to North Carolina.

Oh. Her girlfriend. Is moving. To our state.

A few months ago, Rachel quit her farm job, moved to some town in Georgia, and returned to graphic design or some shit like that. I do not mean to disparage her; I'm sure she's very nice and a great partner to Chris and blah blah blah, but there was something about Rachel being hours away that protected the sacredness of my own relationship with Chris.

Chris does not tell me if Rachel is getting her own place or moving in with her. It doesn't matter, I suppose. I still have brain cancer, and everyone is moving on and around without me.

It's almost as if I'm already dead; I'm watching my family and friends do what they have always done, act as they have always acted, but I am either silent or moving backward. Teaching myself how to walk again. Learning to use my right hand. Trying to remember the difference between Tuesday and Wednesday. And everyone else is working, moving, and only thinking of me in the quiet moments when nothing else is happening around them.

Part of me wishes I was already dead. I still fear the unknown, the continued process and presence of dying. Will my cats be with me? Will I be in the hospital? My parents' house?

It is inevitable, unstoppable.

I immediately block Chris from all social media. This is immature, I know, and I also know this will hurt her the most. I want to hurt her; I want to make her feel as badly as I do. I want someone to feel what I am feeling instead of looking at me with pity or sadness. I want Chris to regret dumping me, regret moving on, regret forgetting about me so she could sleep with some stupid girl with fake freckles and eyebrows that looked as if she drew them on with a permanent marker.

(This was not Rachel but a girl Chris slept with once. Chris claims we were broken up at the time, but we were not. I also suppose that having brain cancer makes me some sort of unreliable narrator, so there's that. Believe whatever you would like, but Chris has a way of making timelines work in her favor.)

I never recovered from the fake freckles and marker eyebrows.

Chole also lied to me multiple times about the same girl, so she is really not my favorite.

I don't understand why I don't get to be happy, I text Chris.

I don't either, she responds, and then I yell at her over and over again in text messages she never answers.

boone, north carolina

When will you start teaching again? my dad asks when my parents visit Boone.

In the fall, if I'm alive by then, I say.

I am not joking when I say this. I have resigned myself to dying a few months after treatment, maybe a little bit longer. I fully expect my tumor to return, maybe in the same place, maybe in a different place, but I know that some demon will spray that silly string into my ear, and there the tumor will be again. Science has proven these things. Since I do not have MGMT, I am less likely to respond to my current chemo drug. My age will help me, yes, but I do not expect a miracle.

No one should.

My dad taught middle school social studies for over thirty years. I admired him, even had him for class in sixth grade, but I never desired to go into teaching myself.

No matter how fantastic our parents are, we spend years trying to be everything they are not, yet somehow, most of us becoming replicas of what we have tried so hard to avoid.

I got lucky.

Sometimes after a class did not go well (and yes, I'm speaking about teaching in the past tense...do I have hope I will return? Sure. Do I want to return? Absolutely. I just don't know if I will be able to endure a teaching day when I can barely finish a twenty-minute radiation treatment), I would call my dad and ask for advice. My classes always went relatively smoothly, but when kids would refuse to stop whispering or fail to do well on a set of papers, I would solicit his guidance.

Don't let it get to you, he always said. *Just go in the next day and start over. They will forget. You will forget. Don't let them see that you're worried.*

He was always right. I remember having him in class; everything was perfectly planned, nothing went awry, and he would throw in a joke every two minutes. Kids wanted to please him and never spoke out of turn. My dad has always been soft-spoken but firm; he was the teacher and father no one feared—you just did not want to disappoint him, ever.

This one class never laughs at my jokes, I tell him.

Eh, they probably just don't get them, he says. *Don't worry about it.*

My dad has aged significantly in the past two years. He spent last Christmas in the hospital after ongoing Lyme Disease did not get properly diagnosed. Doctors accused him of having alcohol withdrawals and not understanding how tick bites work. After being on a ventilator and having his weight drop to 97 pounds, he started to improve and feel better.

Now he shuffles around like an old man who forgot his tap shoes, and my mom has to help him up curbs and flights of stairs.

Can you hold my tea? I ask my sister.

She rolls her eyes.

I saw that, I say. *I saw you roll your eyes, Sarah.*

You and Dad make quite the pair, she says.

I feel sorry for her and my mother.

After my parents settle in to their hotel room, my mom, sister, and I head to the indoor pool while Dad watches NASCAR. I didn't realize he was a NASCAR fan; Sarah tells me that *this all just started within the last year.*

It's funny how illness changes us, I think.

I started being even more of a cunt, and Dad started watching NASCAR.

comfort suites, boone, north carolina

Once in the pool, my mom and her polka dot tankini corner me and Sarah into the shallow end.

I thought the water would be warmer once I dipped my shoulders under, but I continue to shiver. Sarah's arms look like chicken thighs, and I snicker.

I just want to ask you both how you think you get to heaven, my mom says.

Oh god.

I answer reflexively. It's not that I believe or disbelieve the same Jesus my mom adores, but I do not have enough energy to argue or even listen. I want to continue attempting to kick my legs in the pool; kicking is an act I have struggled with, but shoving my legs and knees behind me and upward is much easier while in water.

You have to be saved, I say.

And then what? my mom asks.

I just don't see why we all can't be good people and get to heaven, my sister says. *Plus, I don't believe in hell. And who created God? Why can't anyone answer my questions?*

I am not allowed to be in the pool. Doctors fear I will have another seizure and drown, or some shit like that. I do not care; I knew my mom and sister would be with me, and I did not plan on going underwater.

Now, I wish I could dunk myself away from this conversation.

Do you know who Satan was? my mom asks. I know she will tell us; she does not want us to answer. *He was a praise and worship leader in God's choir. He got too much power, and it went to his head.*

This explains so much, I say as I raise my knees in the water. I almost fall over. *I know many praise and worship leaders this could describe.*

My mom laughs, but Sarah has not finished.

I bet you think Jesus had blond hair and blue eyes, right? Do you think Earth is flat?

No, my mom answers.

It says Earth is flat in the Bible. That's why we have all these crazy folks running around pretending like Earth is flat! IT SAYS SO IN THE BIBLE.

Oh, it does not, my mom says.

Have you read the entire Bible? Sarah speaks to my mom but splashes me with water. *That's what I thought.*

I do not want to agree or disagree with either one of them, but I find that I want to say something, want to describe my ideas of balance.

If there's a heaven, then there has to be a hell, I say.

Yeah, and we're living in it right now, bitches! Sarah says as she pirouettes away in the water.

Maybe she's right, I think. Although both Sarah and Chris have both discussed with me the possibility of my soul somehow choosing the path of type one diabetes and brain cancer for myself (as a challenge? as a chance to right some wrong I committed in a past life?), I am less convinced. I would have never chosen this, and I do not know why anyone would have volunteered for diabetes and brain cancer in the same lifetime.

I would not have picked either of them.

I would not have chosen this.

Any of this.

boone, north carolina

I'm going to plan a cruise for us after I retire, my mom says.

When do you retire? I ask.

Not this March but the next, my mom says.

I'll be dead by then, I say.

Oh, you will not. That's just what you read on the internet.

Well, true.

But I supplemented the Wikipedia articles and forum posts with scholarly journals and academic articles that were all in agreeance: 12 to 15 months. That's the median survival rate, but most glioblastoma patients fail to live longer than a year after diagnosis, surgery, and treatment. A few live for about another three years, and an even smaller amount thrive past five years.

My sister seems to have accepted this and laughs at my dying jokes. I am certain my father has no idea what is happening, and my mom seems as in denial now as she was when she believed my tumor was an abscessed tooth.

Maybe I'll ask if I can borrow against my retirement, my mom says. *You know, get the money early so we can take a cruise this summer and not wait until next March.*

She is not in denial, I think. She is just afraid I know the truth, afraid I know what might actually happen next.

boone, north carolina

We take our parents to a diner beside their hotel.

Mom, who can sometimes eat gluten and sometimes not, orders everything a la carte, although I'm relatively sure there is a numbered meal with all of the same items she ordered.

How would you like your eggs? the server, a bearded kid who looks like every other bearded kid in Boone, asks her.

She points a manicured finger in the air toward the kid.

Do you scramble?

Embarrassed, I stare at the marbled, glittery table. I am as pink as the neon sign above the framed Elvis record.

Jesus, Mom, of course they scramble. It's a diner, Sarah says.

She's always been braver with our mom than I have been.

Well, I didn't know.

And for you, sir? the server asks our father.

Mumbleplaincheeseburgermumblemumblefriescough.

What was that, sir?

He wants a plain cheeseburger with fries, my sister says.

My sister thinks the sun is a hologram, yet she has more sense than any of us at the table.

I eat half my meal and let the rest go cold.

Sarah finishes my biscuit and gravy. My mom makes me eat her gluten-free fruit that she refuses to touch. There is nothing wrong with it; I think she knew I would want it. I eat a grape and one piece of pineapple, and I am done.

I have no appetite for anything, scrambled or otherwise.

boone, north carolina

February 18th marks two months since my craniotomy.

I haven't heard from Feeney in weeks.

Maybe she is giving me my space.

Some friends have disappeared? Are giving me space? Always hated me and needed an excuse to get rid of me?

I am not sure.

Feeney.

I don't know where some of my friends have gone. I think about texting her, but I do not. I have no idea what my responsibilities as a friend are anymore.

boone, north carolina

Yesterday in the shower, I pulled chunks of hair from my side ponytail. This was not supposed to happen; the hair came from the side of my head that never had a tumor, the side of my head where I kept my hair in the first place. I was not supposed to lose any hair from *the good side*, but I watch it swirl down the shower drain as if it never knew me at all.

How long have you been with me, hair? At least a few years?

Yeah, well, fuck you too.

boone, north carolina

My cats, Pru and Duffles, never leave my side.

Duffles cries when she sees me use my shower chair for the first time. Cats have emotions and feelings; most people do not realize their capacity to love.

Duffles watches me attempt to maneuver myself from the edge of the shower bench and into the tub. The bench sets both in and outside the shower, so I do not have to step over the bath to get into the water.

Showers are such a luxury. I learned this in the hospital when I was not permitted to have one for days. Before my seizure and craniotomy, I showered twice a day: before I went to school and after I got home from the gym. After surgery, I could not wash my hair because of the staples. My sister did it for me once; we discovered you can get away with a lot in the neurology unit. There are so many patients and not enough nurses to keep a consistent watch on everyone. Once at the rehabilitation center, I could not take a step from the bed to the bathroom without a nurse receiving an audial notification of some sort.

Showers at home are less of a luxury, but I do not forget.

Duffles has never seen me struggle.

I have always been her mom, her cuddle buddy, her world.

After crying at my inability to simply step into the shower, Duffles sits on the sink and watches me. She wants to make certain I do not fall or misstep and hurt myself. She observes me getting dressed and watches with care as I struggle to get my right leg into my pants.

Pru has different issues.

She would not let anyone touch her while I was away in the hospital. She hid behind the water heater and under the bed. She hissed at friends who came over to feed them and refused to bathe herself until I came home.

Now Pru sleeps beside me and puts one paw on my arm or my chest as I try to rest. Her purr keeps me awake, but I do not mind.

If I am awake, I know I am alive.

boone, north carolina

I tend to wake up around 3:30 or 4:30 a.m. with chemo nausea. I cannot remember the last time I had a bowel movement. I kept track of things like this in the hospital; I had nothing else to do. Now I can barely remember to give my insulin and take the fistfuls of pills I need to kill the cancer and keep my mood consistent.

The nausea smells like loneliness and sadness.

I am not strong; I am not brave.

I am a 36-year-old with brain cancer and type one diabetes who feels tired of fighting.

boone, north carolina/the dash

Shave the whole thing, I tell Sarah as I thrust a handful of dark hair at her. She sits outside my apartment, smoking a cigarette by the river and looking effortlessly hip in her torn black jeans and pink shirt.

If you let me look at it when it's dry, I can figure out where it's falling out. Maybe we won't have to shave it.

I want to shave it, I say. I drop the hair onto the pavement, and the wind carries the strands toward the water.

Mermaid wig material.

I mean, if you want, I'll shave my head with you, she says.

I don't need solidarity.

Thank god, she says as she smashes the cigarette into a rock. *I've been trying to grow mine out.*

We laugh.

By the way, she says. *Mom is worried about you. She doesn't like when you joke about dying. I told her she should be happy you are joking; if you weren't joking, you would be crying.*

This is true, I say. *I might as well joke about it. If I didn't, it wouldn't be me.*

Let's do a makeover, Sarah says. *I need to practice my makeup skills.*

Fine.

We go inside. My one-bedroom apartment has gotten cozier since Sarah moved in; she has the living room and kitchen, while I sleep in the bedroom. There is less space but more love. I never hear her go to the bathroom, but she locks the door when she does. Habit, she says. For someone with a career in appearance, I am always surprised at her modesty.

I sit and face the dishwasher, just as JC did the other night. The best lighting. At first, Sarah takes scissors to the right side of my head. She cuts and chops without resolution or design. If she did not have a job as a stylist in Brooklyn, I would be worried.

This is so fun, she says.

Dear god.

The clippers buzz, and I have a short flashback to moments before brain surgery when I wondered if I would be able to hear, to feel anything.

I started down the middle so you can't change your mind, Sarah says.

I don't want to change my mind. I am not attached to my hair. I only had one side of hair, anyway, and I always pulled it up into a man bun or ponytail. I was more alarmed at losing chunks of it in the shower, when I brushed it, and when I tried to untangle the ends.

No one tells you that the hair falls out root-to-tip and in clumps that resemble extensions that some people pay hundreds of dollars to tape onto their heads. I imagined my hair coming out in strands, in short little clips, but I did not realize the strands would disembody themselves from my scalp as if it never belonged there at all.

I look fucking badass with a shaved head.

Comments:

I think you were meant to have a shaved head.

You have a nicely-shaped head.

I didn't realize there were people without nicely-shaped heads?

You were cute before, but you're even cuter now with a shaved head.

I like that one the best.

Sarah drops me off in The Dash that night so I can make an early appointment the next morning. I take my cat Prufrock with me; I am the only one she will allow to give her the hyperthyroidism pill she just started taking, so she must accompany me everywhere.

I do not mind.

The next morning, I crate Pru so she will not escape.

I request an Uber.

The Uber driver tries to drop me off at the children's hospital.

I laugh I laugh I laugh.

I have to about these things.

the hawthorne hotel, the dash

Pru likes looking out the window of the hotel.

After radiation treatment, I come back and open the blinds. The window frames the parking lot and brief clips of Winston-Salem traffic.

I feel as if I have seen the city from every angle; every room I have slept in, every window I have stared past, has shown something different, something new. Compared to Boone, the landscape in The Dash is as flat as my survival chances.

Pru and I look out the window together and pretend we see mountains.

See? I tell her. *Just like home. Look at all the pretty green trees and hills out there.*

She purrs as if she believes me.

I almost believe myself.

wake forest baptist hospital, comprehensive cancer center, the dash

I am selected to be interviewed for a study examining cancer patients between the age of 25 and 39. The focus of the study is fertility and body image.

Patient 1301A.

How has your cancer diagnosis affected your thoughts on fertility? the interviewer asks.

It has not. I never wanted children.

Has your cancer diagnosis affected the way your partner feels about fertility?

Ha. No. What?

Have you changed your views about having children since your diagnosis?

I mean, look. I never wanted children. Some people don't. I never did. Just never thought of it as *a thing*, you know? Most of my friends don't have or want children. Sure, some people, some women my age, might struggle with this sort of problem, but I haven't. I could see some women who wanted to have kids receiving my diagnosis and being devastated, but that's just not me.

I'm sorry to waste your time.

I'm basically just here for the $50 gift card.

Do you live alone?

Yes.

Are you alone?

The interviewer does not ask this, but I feel as if I can read her mind.

Let's move to the body image portion of the interview.

Great.

How has your body image changed since your diagnosis?

I have always been short and curvy. That hasn't changed. Do I like that? I don't know. It's what I have. I can't hate it. I had half my head shaved before the diagnosis, so losing the other half didn't seem like a big deal. I could see how some people…

You keep mentioning some people.

Well, I mean, I just haven't had a hard time with body image. It's been more of an emotional mindfuck, more than anything.

What's your highest level of education?

Ph.D.

Do you avoid certain people because you fear your body has changed?

Oh. Right. A lot has changed.

I had forgotten.

I played roller derby. It's hard for me to let my teammates see me when I'm having trouble walking…but my walking has really improved over the past two months, so it's, like, not even really a thing anymore, but it's…weird. Sometimes I use a walker, sometimes I use a cane, sometimes I use nothing at all. Still kinda weird.

I am certain this lady hates me.

Tell me more about your trouble walking.

I remember the first time I walked in the neurology unit with the help of a physical therapist. I had tried to walk on my own, but I found out—rather quickly—that you're not supposed to do that. The physical therapist put a tall mirror in front of me, and it was the first time I had seen myself since surgery. I hadn't looked in the mirror because I didn't want to see the staples in my head; I didn't want to see how the surgery had changed me. So, I was trying to walk with a walker, and I thought I was walking normally, but when I pulled my head up and looked in the mirror, I was dragging my right leg completely behind me. It was like it didn't even belong to my body any longer. And I wasn't even putting any pressure on the walker with my right hand because it didn't really work that well either. A month earlier I was flying around a rink on roller skates smacking into people with my hips, and then I can't even walk. Within a day, everything was gone.

That shook me.

Do they have roller derby teams around here?

The closest team is Greensboro, but they are everywhere. You just have to know where to look for them.

Is there anything else you want us to know about body image or fertility?

I mean, I would like to know if there are other people out there like me. I mean, surely I'm not the only 36-year-old with some sort of cancer. I just haven't seen anyone my age around here, hardly ever. They are all in their 60s or 70s. I mean, not to be crass, but Jesus. There have to be other people like me, right? I guess that's not really answering your question, but I have found that there is a lack of resources concerning young women and cancer.

Do you mind if I give your name and contact information to some people?

Of course not.

I want to talk.

I want to see exactly what is going on with them.

I want to feel less isolated.

I want to feel like I belong somewhere.

This concludes our interview. I will now turn off the recorder.

the dash

When the second Uber driver drops me off at the children's hospital, I start to wonder if the fully-shaved head was a bad idea.

the hawthorne, the dash

When I feel the sickest, I text Alex.

I don't know why, exactly, except that I had the dream about her where she whispered to me that *everything would be okay*, and I felt comforted in a way that I didn't when other people told me. I shared this with Alex, and she seemed to accept this, to claim this, so I feel comfortable.

I am fully walking without assistance, but I still have a lot of weakness in my right side. I often feel like my body isn't mine.

I also feel like this when I am standing over the toilet hoping to vomit, but I do not mention this. The nausea tends to envelop me, to consume me. I never force myself to puke because I do not want to make the situation worse for myself. I am afraid if I vomit, I will never stop.

Instead, I collapse in bed like a foldable doll and reach out.

It's kinda like my body dysmorphia, but not at all, she responds.

This is why I text her. She can connect with me without claiming to understand my experience. There is hardly anything worse than the phrase *I understand*. No, you don't understand. Not at all. This phrase is only made worse if followed up by *I understand because my grandfather…I understand because my sister's husband's third cousin…I understand because I had a cancer scare once when I thought I found a lump in my breast…*

…no.

You do not understand.

Alex never claims to understand but can connect to my experience through her own.

This is my favorite element of human nature.

I do not understand but I can try.

I do not understand but I can connect.

I do not understand but I can hope.

the pawthorne (Pru's name for the hotel), the dash

I run out of turkey during our third day in the hotel.

The cat is upset.

I am a terrible mother, but I think she might understand.

I wonder what, I wonder how my sister is doing in Boone, all alone except for the other pets.

wake forest baptist hospital, comprehensive cancer center, the dash

Fourteen.

The number of staples I had in my head.

My fourteenth day of radiation treatment.

My leg falls asleep, and then it twitches like a tree branch in quick wind.

Sometimes I cannot tell if I am about to have another seizure or if I am just tired. Or scared. Or insane.

Hyperaware, maybe.

There is a new technician this morning, and she is in training. My regular *radie ladies* have given her the opportunity to attempt all procedures herself, and this makes me nervous.

Twitchy.

You are a teacher, I remind myself. *She has to learn.*

She is very sweet and trying oh-so-hard. She is nervous; I can tell by the way she fails to answer questions that the experienced radie ladies ask her.

Do you need to move her shoulders more toward you or more toward me?

Umm…

Look at the ceiling.

We all look at the ceiling.

I have no choice.

the road

When we make the nearly two-hour drive to radiation on weekday mornings, Sarah and I listen to music we liked in our mid-20s. There is not only something nostalgic about this, but also something that makes me feel like I am still alive. Something that makes me feel like I am making it. Something that makes me feel as if I am not done, not quite yet.

Old 97s. The Jayhawks. Ryan Adams.

These three appear on our playlists frequently.

I went out with my friend Lindsay before I left New York, and he was surprised at the type of music I like.

Cause she looks all punk and stuff.

Not the type of girl who would listen to alternative country music, though she has been wearing a flannel since she's been in Boone.

She looks like Lori Petty in *Tank Girl* but acts like Lori Petty's character in *Orange is the New Black*, especially when she wants to talk about those damn conspiracy theories.

It's all about crisis acting. I'm not saying these things didn't happen—because I would feel like an asshole if they did—but I'm just saying that the same kid involved in crisis b was also in a video for crisis a, and there is footage—actual footage!—of him fucking up his lines! And there is no fucking way we have actually been to space. There is this report where this dude needed to use a space suit for protection against something, and he called someone who worked for NASA because he thought, hey, that would be the best protection, right? And, by the way, everyone who works for NASA is an ex-convict, just in case you were wondering. Anyway, the guy who worked for NASA said the spacesuits would not protect anyone from anything, so obviously, we never made it to the moon. And, according to reports, there was a button on The Challenger that anyone could press whenever that would blow up the whole shebang. NASA is WHACK. Oh, and also, the Boston Marathon bombing? That guy who was on Oprah afterward totally lost his legs in Iraq, not in the bombing. He was, like, doing wheelies and shit in his wheelchair four days after the bombing incident. There is no way that shit is real.

I don't know how to respond, so I just start playing music from my phone.

Old 97's. The Jayhawks. Ryan Adams.

I don't want the conspiracy theory conversation to veer into how cancer is not real and how my doctors have given me false MRIs in attempt to get money from me.

Right now, I am still alive. I am still making it. I am not a crisis actor. I am not done, not quite yet.

boone, north carolina

My butthole hurts.

These are the things no one tells you.

Partly, the reason for this memoir is to tell everyone what no one else wants to say. To give a raw account of what having cancer, specifically brain cancer, is like. There are other reasons for this memoir, of course, such as giving myself something to do to make certain my brain still functions in some way.

I did not have a bowel movement for about two weeks, but it wasn't something I thought about until my doctor asked me.

Doctors and nurses love these conversations.

They give me some type of stool softener, and three hours later, my stomach wrings itself out in the toilet, and I finally feel like I might be dying.

When I wipe my ass, there is nothing but blood.

boone, north carolina

I now have crop circles on my shaved head.

I don't think anyone can see them unless I bend over.

I hope not.

the road

Sarah decides to take my car back to New York. The tiny purple Scion needs new tires, an oil change, and an inspection, so we complete this before she leaves. The mundane details of everyday life. I do not know how I managed to pay for all this and not have the opportunity to drive the car myself, but this is my existence now. I have lost control of each step, of every normality.

She will drop me off in The Dash before she leaves, and I will stay at The Hawthorne for over two weeks, until my radiation is complete. With generous donations people have given me, I have enough money for this. I've rarely had enough money to stay one or two nights in a hotel, and suddenly, I can stay for half a month and probably order room service if I want.

During lunch, Sarah begs me not to leave her.

You can't leave me alone with Mom and Dad. They're too crazy. You can't do it, SZ.

She looks at me desperately over the plate of garlic bread sticks.

I wish I could promise her something; I wish I could promise her anything.

I imagine her life without me, our mom constantly texting and calling her to make sure she's on the train or at work or back at home. She does not do this to her now, but I can imagine her doing this once I am dead. Never leaving Sarah alone, sending her those weird Facebook chain mail messages about love and motherhood and sadness. Making her come home for holidays and sit on the blue kitchen chairs and eat hash brown casserole that should have been left in the oven a little bit longer. Talking about how if I was there, if I was still around, I would have wanted a grilled chicken salad with pineapple for dinner, but now that I wasn't there, now that I wasn't around, they would just eat the hash brown casserole for all meals.

Or maybe they wouldn't talk about me at all.

Maybe life would go on without me, but there would just be one of us instead of two.

Mom would solicit Sarah to attend church with her on Sunday mornings and Wednesday nights, but Sarah would eventually figure this out and finagle her trips home on weekdays nowhere near Wednesdays or Sundays.

Dad would sit and stare at the birdhouse I gave him for Christmas and think about my birthday, which he marked on his calendar as one of the coldest days of the year. He told me he woke up the morning before my mom gave birth and played the Michael Martin Murphey song "Carolina in the Pines" on his record player as he stared at his own puffs of breath by the woodstove. I suppose my dad was a bit of a psychic and somehow knew I would spend the last years of my life in a small mountain town in North Carolina. He would consider this tale, this bit of circular reasoning, while drinking black coffee out of his World's Fair coffee mug that he brought back after living in New York for three months in his early 20s.

Maybe I should have made more mistakes.

Maybe I should have lived in bigger cities.

Maybe I should have slept with more people, but I never really had the chance. I was never the type of woman *people slept with*. Maybe I was too intimidating, too closed off. Maybe I was too good for all of them.

Oh god, I say to Sarah as I bite the head off a breadstick. *I'm sorry.*

I can't tell her I won't leave her. I can't promise I will stick around and help her deal with Mom and Dad as they age and get even more neurotic than they already are, Mom memorizing more quotes from her preacher and Dad mumbling about cheeseburgers in the middle of the day.

Her eyes, which are gray today, continue to beg.

Don't leave me. Don't go.

But I fear I will have no choice, no decision, no way to backtrack on this brain cancer thing that has taken me over suddenly and wholly.

the road

Sarah has one job: to get me to radiation on time. But she wakes up later each morning and spends more time putting her makeup on in the sink while I wait in the car. There is road work today and traffic packed around us like growling cats in cardboard boxes.

I am tired of this.

I am tired of everything.

the dash

Sarah and I decide to stop at a restaurant called Twin Peaks after I finish treatment for the day. We are thrilled to observe a Kyle MacLachlan-inspired lodge and marvel at pictures of Laura Palmer that would surely line the windows in memoriam. The restaurant does not open until 11, so we take selfies with the signs outside.

I am the first one to notice the waitresses dressed in booty shorts and midriff flannels.

Oh no, Sarah says. It seems we made a mistake.

But we are the only people in the restaurant and have been spotted by the scantily-dressed staff.

Just embrace it, I say.

We have no other choice.

boone, north carolina

Conversation with Alex intensifies one afternoon and continues into evening. I am surprised at how quickly we connect and how much we have in common. Alex tells me how she is preparing for gender confirmation surgery and how at one appointment, five doctors stared at her genitals and commented on them as if they were tomorrow's lunch.

I feel sheepish for comparing my own experience, but I am struck by how we both have bodies that at some point, did not or do not feel like our own.

I do not mean to compare, but I do seek to connect.

This reminds me of when I was in the hospital, and I had to have a nurse put my tampon in for me. I never thought there was anything more humiliating than having someone wipe my ass—which also had to happen a bunch—but then Nurse Becky had to stick the fucking thing in, and I thought my life was over. The next time, she watched me insert the tampon with my left hand and guided me through the process. I kept trying to make jokes, but it didn't make the situation any better.

UGH PREACH, Alex responds.

We begin this knowing the end: death, failure, demise. But there would also be closure. Ultimate closure. Alex is prepared for this; I know because she told me she lost 17 people in the last year. She told me she *wanted to take ownership* of my impending death. Sure, she was drunk when she said this, but I needed to let someone else carry my burden of dying.

Alex seemed like the appropriate person.

I do not know how JC feels about any of this.

We have not discussed this at all, though I know JC is aware Alex and I talk.

Would it be so bad to make a connection at this point?

Would it be so bad to begin something new with someone?

Would it be so bad to experience feelings I never thought I deserved to have again?

I walk into the bathroom and press my chin to my chest. I have a bigger crop circle on top of my head where the radiation has done its work. I actually resemble a cancer patient now; before the midway point of radiation, I just looked like a woman with a weird, alternative haircut. Now I look sick. Now I look like I am dying. Now I look like someone who needs some cancer patient headwear, a wrap or rag or hat of some sort.

I look terrible in hats.

Despite the crop circle on my head, I do not feel ugly. I look at myself in the mirror and see strength and pride. When I think back to myself prior to surgery, I remember the thoughts I attempted to reconcile, the thoughts I let rumble in my psyche that no one could soothe. *I can't do surgery. I'm not strong enough. I can't have fucking staples in my head. I can't even look at that shit on television, more or less have it in my own head. I can't I can't I can't.*

And then Jenna told me I could, and I had no choice but to believe her.

I survived.

I never promised to beat cancer or kick cancer's ass or disassemble the statistics to make them fit my own needs and hopes.

But I did wake up in ICU with fourteen staples in my head and felt thirsty and weird and tired; I did not feel sick yet or so grossed out by myself that I could not function. Sure, I refused to look at myself in the mirror, but once I did, I realized the staples looked more like a semi-permanent headband, only slightly Frankenstein-ish, and I could live with waiting for that scar to heal.

And it did heal.

Quickly.

As it turns out, I am perfectly healthy except for brain cancer and type one diabetes.

But anyway.

Alex.

I feel connected to Alex.

I feel comfortable.

I feel as if I can be myself, whether I have staples in my head or crop circles or nothing at all.

boone, north carolina

I wake up and see Sarah has folded my dry clothes. I never thought my little sister, who is a hairstylist in New York City and never gets up before 2 p.m., would be folding my clothes for me.

I rarely folded my own clothes.

I see the clothes after I wake from a nap. I do not really sleep for long amounts of time; I rest for a few hours and then stir from the discomfort and numb pain.

During one of those brief sleeps, I dream I am in JC's kitchen. Nothing significant happens except that I see a card on her fridge with my name on it.

SZ—

the card says,

You are going to be okay.

I wish I believed this. But maybe *okay* does not mean I am going to survive or live or conquer cancer; maybe *okay* means death won't be that scary or that terrifying or that painful. That's what I hope for now; that's what I hope for at this point.

Death with some sort of slow fade.

Death where my head does not feel as if it is going to spontaneously combust.

Because that's what I imagine.

My head just bursting, a new tumor just blowing up inside my skull and killing me as I scream and cry and kick my feet for the final time.

But maybe I will just close my eyes, begin to dream, find myself in JC's kitchen, and never awake again.

wake forest baptist hospital, comprehensive cancer center, the dash

The radie ladies ask me to arrive twenty minutes early.

We are really backed up lately, they say.

I have been watching; three new people arrived yesterday morning for radiation. A young Hispanic man, a middle-aged man who could barely breathe or sit up in his wheelchair, and someone on a hospital bed named Tom.

I only know his name because I watched his wife variate between slumping in a chair and frantically searching the rectangular radiation waiting room looking for him. Once the techs pulled Tom out of the radiation room, the lady asked *Is that Tom Sterling?* and the radie ladies looked terrified of breaking every single HIPAA law by confirming that yes, it was *Tom Sterling* on that stretcher.

His wife ran to be beside him.

Rookies.

My sister came with me on the first day of radiation but drops me off every day after that. She goes to the Shell station and smokes cigarettes with naughty nurses and patients who do not actually give a fuck about their health. Then she sometimes puts on makeup and pulls around to pick me up. No one is chasing me down in the radiation hallway to make sure I get to where I am going.

But I do not need this.

I do not want this.

I am the person they ask to arrive twenty minutes early because they know I can.

You're actually less tired than about 95% of the patients we see here, my radiation oncologist tells me. *You're doing really well.*

I do not know exactly how to take this, but I think she means to compliment me. Dr. Crowder giggles awkwardly; I like her. She is intelligent but seems like someone who might watch *Friends* or *The Wonder Years* with her cat for hours on her days off, if she gets those.

boone, north carolina

I am walking without assistance and haven't thrown up for a few days. I've only had a few bad blood sugars since starting chemo and radiation—one high blood sugar and lows every night around 3 a.m.

Nausea typically accompanies the low blood sugars, which makes it difficult to eat. But I drink a lot of juice and try to eat granola when the drops occur. I guess I've had more than *a few bad blood sugars*, but the lows seem fixable, easy. The high blood sugars make me feel more tired and nauseous and like I actually might be dying.

Sometimes I feel sick sometimes I feel sick sometimes I feel sick.

Yet when I look around me in the radiation hallway, I seem way less sick than those around me. Sure, I have brain cancer, and that brain cancer can only be treated and not cured, but I appear to be doing remarkably well for myself.

No matter how much I try to avoid comparing myself to others, this happens. I look at everyone around me and marvel at my ability to walk into the radiation room without a stretcher, without a wheelchair, and without a walker. I can speak, I can joke with the radie ladies, and I can see myself out when I am done.

Not everyone can be so lucky.

So yes, I can arrive twenty minutes early.

I can do whatever is asked of me.

boone, north carolina

I am packing my new suitcase for my upcoming stay at The Hawthorne in The Dash.

Sarah will drop me off before she takes my car with her to New York. I still have half of my treatments left, but Sarah must return to work.

I have no idea if I have everything I need. So many pill bottles. Extra insulin. Extra underwear. Sweatpants. Something nice in case I decide to leave the hotel room and do something fun.

I probably won't.

I am sitting on the floor.

Before the brain cancer, I was always a floor sitter. I preferred lounging on the floor to read, watch television, or hang out with friends.

And then the floor became an enemy.

After falling in the hospital, once in my snowy driveway, and almost in Food Lion a few hours ago, I decide I do not like the floor quite as well.

But now I am sitting on the floor, trying to finish packing my suitcase.

Wheel of Fortune is on the television.

Do you have an internal alarm that goes off whenever Wheel of Fortune is on TV? Sarah asks me. *Because you always seem to know right when it's about to come on.*

I do not think Sarah likes *Wheel of Fortune*, but she indulges me. We watch a lot of shitty television: Lifetime movies, reality television shows, and the Game Show Network. She sits on the wooden dining room chair I dragged to my room, and I am usually on the bed.

The cancer bed.

But tonight, I am sitting on the floor.

After I close my suitcase, I attempt to stand. Instead, I tip over toward the television table and fall onto my right shoulder. I am not hurt; I am not even embarrassed, although maybe I should be.

Help! I say. *I've fallen in the park, and I can't get up!*

Sarah and I see the Life Alert commercial at least four times a day. I remember this commercial from when we were children, teenagers maybe. I do not think they have changed the script or the actors since then, except they definitely added the scene where the guy falls in the park.

Sarah laughs and takes a drink of her Mountain Dew slushie. Sarah is happier when she has caffeine and sugar.

I have learned this.

She makes no move to help me up, but she keeps laughing and snorts a bit of Mountain Dew slushie out her nostril.

Goddammit, that burned, she says.

Help! I've fallen in the park, and I can't get up! I say.

My therapists at the rehabilitation center attempted to convince me to order a Life Alert before I left the Sticht Center; my mom supported the idea, but I refused. I am 36-years-old, the fire department is across the street from my apartment, and I have a cell phone. These were my reasons.

Now, on the floor and knowing my sister will leave in three days, I wonder if maybe I should have ordered one. One for the shower. One for my neck. One for walks in the park.

Are you okay, for real? my sister asks. *You were really close to hitting your head on the table.*

I pull myself upward. I still have a relatively strong core, even if I have not exercised in two months.

I'm fine, I say, and I am. *But I don't think you should leave me.*

I don't think I should either, she says, and I cannot tell if she is joking or serious.

Neither of us solve the final *Wheel of Fortune* puzzle that night.

BABY GROUNDHOGS.

Who could ever get that? I ask.

I really don't know. That's so obscure, Sarah says.

I feel like they are making the puzzles a lot harder lately because they are running out of money or something, I say. *They are tired of giving out $35,000 every other night.*

I stand up from the ground.

You're going to be okay, Sarah says, but I am not certain she has convinced herself, not actually.

boone, north carolina

I go as a spectator to the first roller derby bout of the season.

The first person I see is Feeney.

My seizure buddy.

The one who brought an actual wreath to me in the neurology unit on Christmas day, even though she was spending the day with her family and loved ones.

She made time for me.

Recently, Feeney was supposed to bring over some kind of broth, but I did not hear from her. She said she would be over on Friday, but I never received a call, never received a text. Nothing. She may have forgotten; I am surprised I did not forget.

Some people disappear.

I knew this; I was told this.

Feeney and I spent so much time together throughout the week, before the disagreement, before the seizure.

We give each other a brief hug. I think she may be afraid of me now. The seizure, the medical part, the brain surgery she could handle. Now that she sees me without hair, without spirit, she cannot stand to see the weakness. It reminds her that this could happen to anyone; this could happen to her.

Cancer could happen to anyone.

We talk about how she stayed up until 3:30 a.m. to finish the bout programs. Derby takes up much more time than just skating around on a track and hitting people. The team does everything from preparing the bout space to advertising to creating the artwork and programming for the event.

Perhaps this explains why she forgot to come over. She was busy. This makes sense—this makes me feel less like she fears me.

As the bout begins, I watch my friends skate. I feel pride for each wheel that spins in front of another—I smile when our team leads and panic when they fall behind. The game is tight and unpredictable. The score changes each jam, and players from both teams land without remorse in the penalty box.

I wish I was skating, but I am nearly too tired to even consider how it might feel to gear up and tie my boots up to my ankles.

I watch my friends roll around the rink and smack their shoulders and hips into the opposing team. I cringe when my former teammates elbow others or accidentally trip other skaters; as a skater, I never accrued many penalties. I may not have been the biggest body or the hardest hitter, but I skated cleanly each bout.

The game comes down to the final jam. The opposing team's jammer goes to the box, which means my team could catch up and ostensibly win the bout. I want my team to win so badly. For a few moments, I forget about cancer. I forget I am likely dying; I forget I may not ever attend another bout again. I watch my team's jammer—PYT—attempt to lap the opposing team's blockers and earn enough points to tip the score in our favor.

But things do not go as planned.

If anything, I've learned nothing goes as planned. You have to take detours and do things you do not expect and hope for the best. Even then, we all still die or lose or come up empty in some way.

PYT gives the jam everything she can. I can feel her fighting. I can feel her pushing through the tough blockers. I can feel each pop to the chest she receives, and I only breathe when she begins passing the blockers who attempt to destroy her on the track.

But it's not enough. PYT's offensive blockers cannot give her the appropriate help or prevent the opposing jammer from blowing by once she exits the box. There is nothing that anyone can pinpoint that *went wrong.*

The right things just did not happen when they should have. A bad combination of chance and luck.

PYT exits the track disappointed. It's not her fault, though. Roller derby happens over the span of two thirty-minute halves, so no one can blame the final jammer for the final score. The opposing team wins by nine points, which is nothing in roller derby.

Nine points.

Roller derby is close to an exact science, close to medicinal, close to killing a brain tumor.

Each point is hard earned and projected onto the screen after won. Everyone must fight until the end, and then sometimes, you still lose.

But it's important, it is vital, and it is necessary to never quit moving or pushing or trying.

I think of the red numbers projected onto the ceiling during radiation and wonder how much of my head, my scalp, my brain will survive the daily microwaving sessions.

I am too tired to stand from the inflatable gray couch.

I want to give high-fives to the opposing team and my own team, but I am too slow to reach the track in time. I catch a few stray skaters at the end and smile. I want them to know how proud I am, how much I enjoyed the game, and how much I still admire their strength and skill, even if just a few months earlier, I was doing the same thing myself.

nowhere

Cancer is waiting.

Cancer is waiting in rooms full of sick people who do not all look or act sick; cancer is waiting in rooms full of sick people who *do* look and act sick; cancer is waiting and wondering how long you can avoid looking and acting and feeling sick because maybe, just maybe, you will get lucky and quietly pass away before you need six IVs and a breathing mask and pins stuck in your head like some angry bitch's voodoo doll.

Cancer is waiting in the parking lot of a hotel owned by the hospital because your sister has to drop you off so you can stay at this hotel and Uber to the hospital each morning for treatments because you still cannot legally or physically drive. Cancer is waiting because the hotel room isn't ready but your sister has to go back to New York City and live her punky glamorous lifestyle as a stylist at a high-end grunge boutique. She's been with you for about a month, but she could not stay any longer. She folded your clothes, she drove you everywhere, and she brought you pizza in bed when you felt too tired to put both feet on the floor.

Cancer is waiting to hear when you get your next MRI so you can see if that fucking brain tumor has started to grow back. Cancer is waiting to see what the hell is going on because your foot keeps experiencing spasms in the middle of the night, and you're not certain if it's from swelling, the tumor's return, or just some weird, shitty side effect of the tens of pills you take each day.

Cancer is waiting.

Cancer is waiting to take you away from your teaching career, your roller skating hobby, and your time drinking craft beer with friends. Cancer is waiting to make you trip up the stairs after class, to make you wonder why at 36, your right foot feels completely numb and prevents you from leaving a table after an awkward date. Cancer is waiting to whisk you two hours from your home and let a ginger-bearded surgeon you've never met saw through your skull and yank out a grade IV glioblastoma that sits and waits until the end of the December and beginning of January holidays to let everyone know that *yes, it is fucking malignant* and *no, there is no cure*, and *goddammit, this really fucking sucks because now everything is urgent and everything is possible and everything must happen right now.*

Cancer is fucking waiting, bitches.

It is waiting for everyone, anyone.

Cancer is waiting to take your sister away from her job for a month so she can come and help you get out of bed each morning; cancer is waiting so your sister can wash your hair for you and make certain those fourteen staples from the craniotomy you just had do not get wet, but you can still feel clean because right now, at this very moment, you feel dirty and gross and disgusting. Your sister will drive you four hours a day without complaint because that's what you need, because you have to be at radiation treatments every single weekday and no, you cannot do them where you live because they do not have the proper equipment, so yes, you have to, you must, make that four-hour roundtrip drive each morning because otherwise, your life expectancy dwindles down to weeks instead of months.

Cancer is waiting to surprise five rooms full of students who expected you to walk in and teach a writing class focused on true crime, but instead, someone else comes through the door, and the students can never understand why. A few of them email you because they had you for their first college writing class last semester, but you do not email them back because you just have no idea how to explain that you have brain cancer and cannot be there this semester and may not be there ever again. You do not tell your colleagues the true seriousness of the cancer diagnosis because you so desperately want to return to class, so desperately want to walk those hallways again and spend your lunch working on flash fiction stories and meeting with students about their upcoming projects, but *it just doesn't look that good*, and you have no idea how to say that without sounding tired, weak, defeated.

Cancer is waiting to make you sob as you look at your four-year-old cat and realize she will need to find another mom, and no, no other mom will cuddle her the way you do or make sure that she laps water out of a special Starbucks mug each morning or eats her food on the table so the dog cannot bother her. Cancer is waiting to kill you, and the cat is not a human and cannot be reasoned with and therefore, will not understand why you left her and why you didn't come home one day and why you suddenly disappeared and she never saw you again.

Cancer waits.

It fucking waits.

Cancer waits for your friends to become angry with you because they feel as if you *are shutting them out*. Cancer waits for you to tell your life story and diagnosis to strangers in an Uber because you owe them nothing and they owe you nothing and if you had never met, life would still pretty much be the same and without many other ripples in the greater universe. Cancer is waiting for those friends to wonder why you do not respond to their text messages as quickly as you once did. It's not that you do not want to respond, but the brain surgery and the chemo has *made you forgetful, dammit*, and sometimes you just cannot remember to respond to a question about when you will be in town, when you will be gone for another few weeks of treatment, or where you will be living for the next two weeks.

Cancer is waiting to make you funny.

Cancer is waiting for you to make jokes online about staying alive until the annoying *Jeopardy!* contestant named Alan is ousted from his trivia throne. He makes stupidly irritating finger points toward his daily total when the show begins, and he puts exclamation marks around his entire name as if that makes him more memorable. Well, it does. It makes him more memorable in a palpably negative way, and your online friends think you are funny for making such a terrible joke about staying alive until Alan is done.

Cancer is waiting for your mother to find your sense of humor about dying extremely off-putting and upsetting. She waits until she can speak with your sister alone and says things like *why is she making such terrible jokes?* and your sister responds *wouldn't you rather her joke about it instead of cry? You know she's got terminal cancer, right? She's going to die. Now she just has to find her own way to deal with it.*

Cancer is waiting.

Cancer is waiting to make certain you know that at the end of your life, you will be alone. Sure, your family will be there, maybe a few friends, but you will not have that great love you read about in those trashy novels you devoured in middle school. You will not have a soulmate holding your hand at the end and promising to *see you again one day real soon.* Cancer is waiting to make sure you have a string of ex-lovers acting and reacting in all sorts of strange ways to somehow make themselves feel better about your bad situation. For instance, some will block you on Facebook—even though you are not speaking to them or inviting them back into your life—some will speak to you as if you are still dating—even if they have moved on and are dating someone else—and some will not speak to you at all. Cancer is waiting to make certain you know the difference, because for some reason this will become important, since you will want to divide people into binaries of *good versus bad* even though you never believed in any sort of binaries until now.

Cancer is waiting waiting waiting.

Cancer is waiting to wake you up at 3:30 a.m. and tell you that you really need to puke, but you won't be able to because who knows why. You think of forcing yourself to throw up, but you do not want to make the situation way worse than it needs to be, so you just sit in bed uncomfortably, take a tincture of marijuana oil, and hope for the feeling to pass like a shadow in the hotel dark. Cancer is waiting to make you feel as if you might die in the middle of the night with no warning; cancer is waiting to snatch you up like a nightmare.

You can never wake up, never again.

Cancer is waiting to create chasms within relationships, within friendships, within songs you once heard and thought nothing of how the verse connected to the chorus. Cancer causes that friend to stop texting you, that friend who once went to the gym with you every day. You can't really walk anymore, so what fun would you be at the gym?

Cancer is waiting to do all this.

Every single bit of it.

Cancer is waiting to make you wonder…should I write letters to my loved ones? Should I make videos? As you flop on the radiation table and look at the butterfly stickers on the machine, you think about how letters would be more personal and something they could keep, but your hand hurts too much to make this happen. Sure, your hand works now, kind of, but it aches and screams when you use it too much, which means writing nothing more than ten words with one of the cool pens your well-meaning friend brought you.

Cancer is waiting to make you dread each hour, each minute, each second because how will you fill your time until the end? You thought you would want to do all these cool things before you died, like visit the Grand Canyon or eat pot brownies in Portland or fly to Italy to see your old roller derby teammate. But now you're just fucking tired and can't fucking walk and can do nothing but sit and type this memoir that will exist only unto itself because that is what it is meant to do.

Writing is meant to give you something to do, something to look forward to, something to complete.

You decide to make videos for your friends and family. Little recordings they can watch when they miss you. Should you text them out minutes before you die? Will you actually be able to do this? What if you make the videos and then no one receives them or sees them or gets the chance to hear your final words? What if you give your sister your phone password and task her with sending out the videos and she gets confused or forgets?

You must make them and send them out days before you die.

If the online guide is true, then this will be around the time when you start asking to pack your bags and take a trip somewhere. Time to go. Time to get out. Time to be free.

Cancer is waiting.

Cancer is always waiting.

wake forest baptist hospital. comprehensive cancer center, the dash

On my 19th day of treatment, the machine breaks.

I do not know exactly what happens or why; I am still bolted to the table through my mask. The beeps are shrill and sound like a fire alarm. The radie ladies flip switches and make jokes about how I *broke the machine*. Although I have not panicked during a single treatment, something about the noise and the movement and the feeling of helplessness causes my hands to shake. I want to lift off my mask and run out. I do not care about treatment any longer and look forward to closing my eyes and never waking again.

It occurs to me: I forgot to take my antidepressant this morning.

Does the antidepressant work?

It does not cure brain cancer.

But perhaps it helps my mood.

Stay positive, SZ. Sometimes I cannot tell if I am taking the advice of others or repeating these words to myself in hopes I may believe them someday.

I want to escape the fire alarm; I want the beeps to end.

We're going to have to go get Todd, one of the radie ladies says, though I can tell this is not the desired outcome. Nobody wants to tell Todd about the broken radiation machine.

The ladies keep flipping switches and moving shit around.

I'm sorry, sweetie, I know that sound is annoying.

But the sound is not annoying: it's terrifying. It's horrifying to remember that these women have bolted my face to a table so they can burn my brain cells and maybe, just maybe, kill the cancer growing and forming beneath my skull.

The scariest part, of course, is that there is no guarantee.

And the machine is broken.

What does that mean? Does *broken* mean it is just going to make some extra noise, or does *broken* mean that I won't get the radiation I need? Or will the machine go insane and give me too much? Will the radiation cover my entire body and just kill me as the radie ladies run out of the room to save themselves?

Jesus.

My leg hurts.

I cannot straighten my knee.

I have not taken a shit for at least a week.

My pants have nearly rolled off my hips.

I need to eat more.

I am withering like a dying flower. I hope someone will press me and keep me forever.

I wish I had taken my antidepressant this morning.

The beeping stops, and no one has to call Todd.

boone, north carolina

My iPhone X no longer recognizes my face. Too much of my hair has fallen out, I suppose. My phone no longer recognizes me, but I still recognize myself. Stubborn. Strong. Dying of cancer.

My mobility comes and goes like good weather. On the sunny days, I can walk without stumbling and my body feels like my own. On cloudy and rainy days, the right side of my body feels like it belongs to someone else.

On these days, I no longer recognize my right half.

I am as unreliable as my iPhone.

boone, north carolina

Never have I ever acquired so many groceries.

My fridge has never seen so much food.

My sister throws out soups, bread, and even some old ravioli.

We try to eat everything, but there is just too much.

We do not know how to handle ourselves.

We are small people.

We do not eat this much food.

We are people you take to a buffet and lose money.

We are lost.

boone, north carolina

Chole blocks me on Facebook. We were not friends, but when I search for her name, nothing appears. They still show up on my sister's account, so I know they did not delete their page.

But why?

Why would it matter if we coexisted on social media but were not friends? Why the need to block me? I have no feelings for Chole, except hatred. I think she is a terrible person. Awful. The worst.

I do not want to contact her.

But because she has blocked me, this makes me think she believes I will try to contact her. That she will again accuse me of harassing her, of not letting go, of holding on.

Mostly, I look up her profile to see what stupid decisions they have made lately.

Recently: two terrible tattoos. One of a cartoon character and the other a hand with an eye in the middle. There is red around the eye, and I cannot tell if it is an infection or part of the tattoo.

That's how bad it is.

She is still dating someone who just graduated from college; I have no idea how young this girl is, but Chole looks old enough to be her parent. I am relatively certain, though, that this girl must be more mature than Chole. She likely thinks Chole is *so cool* because she is a bartender at a dive, because she has a lip ring, and because she is a social media slactivist who posts meme after meme about the unfairness of the world but never actually does anything to change the problems that exist.

That's Chole.

Still blocking people on Facebook and pretending not to care.

boone, north carolina/the hawthorne hotel, the dash
Some mornings I awake before 6 a.m. and forget I have brain cancer.

And then I remember.

I remember when I try to move from my bed and cannot swing my right leg over the side of the mattress.

I remember when I try to walk to the shower and my right leg still drags a bit behind me like a branch stuck to my shoe.

I remember when I cannot step over the bathtub ledge to take a shower and need to grab something on the wall to ensure I do not slip and fall and break my hip like an elderly person.

I remember when Duffles, my youngest cat, walks across my

stomach, and I have to wonder who will be her next mom? Who will pet her exactly the way that I do? Who will put water in a mug for her because that's where she likes it best?

I remember when I walk to the hotel lobby at The Hawthorne and wait for an Uber. I remember when I still have trouble getting in and out of other peoples' cars and my right side freezes and cannot move the way it should, the way it once did. I remember when I sit for too long in a room full of old people and have more trouble than the elderly standing up from my chair and heading to the appointment room where the doctor will ask me *how are things going? What is happening that we need to know? Are you feeling sad, lonely, or depressed?*

Fine, considering the circumstances. Everything. Of course I am.

I remember when I see that I have 654 unread emails from work, and it does not matter if I actually open them and read them. I remember when I delete every single email at once because nothing has anything to do with the classes I do not have this semester, and the two emails I received from former students should have been answered last month, but I never did it.

I remember when my mom texts me about six times a day. This would not be weird for many people, for most people, perhaps, but we never really texted before this. My mom and I coexisted and loved one another from afar, and now she wants pictures of my dinner so she can know for certain that I am eating and not lying about what I consume.

I remember when my sister sends out a message to my friends and announces that *SZ is falling and not telling anyone.* Sure, I lost my balance a couple times, but I did not actually fall. *She thinks granola is dinner and barely eats any meals unless force fed.* To be fair, she reads me this message, so I am not surprised or blindsided when my friends begin texting me and asking what I ate for dinner.

I remember when I cannot fall asleep at night because my right side feels like a dumbbell somehow attached to my hip. I remember when I roll over about sixteen times in an attempt to get comfortable. I remember when I check my phone four times to see if anyone has texted me to check in or see how I'm doing or just say hello.

Sometimes they do and sometimes they don't.

I remember.

I remember when I am living in a hotel room because I need to be at radiation Monday through Friday, and I still cannot drive. I do not think I could physically drive, and I am not legally cleared to drive until June, unless I have another seizure.

I remember when I look at my head in the mirror and see those crop circles cancer has left behind on my alien head.

the hawthorne hotel, the dash

Although my sister shaved my head, lonely specks of hair still gel to the pillowcase each night. When I am home, I do not notice. When I am at the hotel and sleeping before radiation begins, the tiny flecks of black blot the white pillowcase and look like a negative photo of the night sky.

the hawthorne hotel, the dash

On my 17th day of treatment, my pubic hair falls out. I do not know why this happens. No one warned me about this.

the hawthorne hotel, the dash

Jenna and Feeney come to visit on a Thursday evening. I am still at the hotel, and I crate the cats, who came with me, so they will not escape.

Jenna arrives first.

There are two queen beds in my room, but Jenna sits beside me. Her thighs touch my shoulders. I appreciate this. Besides the cats and the radie ladies and the table, I have not touched another living being for at least a week. Jenna feels warm and kind and empathetic.

How are you doing? she asks, and I know she wants the real answer, not the answer of *I'm great, girl! Everything is fantastic! Everyone said I would feel bad, but I feel fine!* Jenna knows me too well for this; she also knows because her mom fought cancer and survived. Jenna understands, though, that every day remains another battle. Cancer does not just go away or disappear. It's a disease that lurks in the shadows, even when it pretends to be gone.

I don't know, I say. *Sometimes I really just don't know. I'm tired all the time. I sleep about fifteen hours a day.*

That's normal, Jenna says. *I mean for someone going through this. You deserve to rest.*

Other than that, I feel okay. The nausea has improved a lot since they gave me new medication. I haven't taken a shit in about a week.

Oh, god, we need Feeney to get you some of that powder she is obsessed with.

Once Feeney made us tea on a derby trip, and Jenna and I spent the next morning shitting in the bathroom for about an hour before the bout.

You know when my mom was doing radiation, she was not functional at this point.

I think Jenna may cry, but she holds herself together. I have rarely seen Jenna break down. Since I have known her, I think I have only seen her cry once, and that was during her period and when she was upset about derby.

She was…really burned and…couldn't really move, she says.

Oh god, I didn't mean to make you emotional, I say.

Everyone is different, she says, and I can tell she is worried that maybe I am not prepared for what comes next, for what may appear in those dark corners.

the hawthorne hotel, the dash

Feeney arrives twenty minutes after Jenna, and she announces herself by shaking the rain off her jacket and onto the hotel carpet. Feeney has presence, panache. When she walks into a room, everyone notices.

It's like a derby trip, Feeney says as she smiles.

It is.

Feeney, Jenna, and I often roomed together for derby bouts and tournaments.

Once I got so drunk that I flopped on Feeney's bed in a wet bathing suit and cried for fifteen minutes because I was sad about some stupid relationship and getting an insulin pump. Jenna held my hand throughout that time, and I was too embarrassed to even look at her.

We've been through a lot together.

I don't know if Feeney ever forgave me for getting her bed so wet.

Hammy needs some of that powder, Jenna says.

Oh, magnesium powder, Feeney says. *There is a Whole Foods about a mile from here.*

Of course, Feeney would know exactly where the nearest Whole Foods is.

Feeney knows everything about food.

If we go to Whole Foods, will you still be awake when we get back? Feeney asks.

I can make no promises.

If you're not, we will jump on you, Feeney says.

A true friend.

I know she is serious; I have seen Feeney jump on plenty of sleeping people.

My teammates disappear into the geometric hallway. The Hawthorne, where I am staying, sits somewhere between *The Shining* and a Wes Anderson film. There is a lot of red, a lot of gold.

Weird, old elevators.

People, smiling, always at their appropriate stations.

I love it.

I fear it.

Jenna and Feeney seem as if they are gone for at least an hour, but they are only gone about forty minutes. I've noticed since *all this cancer shit started*, time has simultaneously slowed and accelerated. I feel the need to work quickly, to *do all the things I need to* super fast, but those little moments seem to stretch into days, years.

Maybe this is what happens at the end, I think, especially if you are young. The seconds layer into days so that it seems as if you have spent more time in the world than what you actually get.

Feeney and Jenna return with teas. They return with powders. They return with soda waters. They return with herbal supplements. They return with kombucha.

You will definitely be able to use the bathroom tomorrow morning, Feeney says as she fixes me a tea. She uses a plastic fork to thrust some magnesium powder into the warm mug.

But...what time? Jenna asks.

I can tell she is worried I will need to take a shit while I am bolted to the radiation table.

Probably when she wakes up, Feeney says. *What time do you wake up?*

I have been waking up around 5:30 a.m.

I just don't want her to... Jenna says.

Oh, you're worried that she'll have to go when...

No one wants to say *when she's bolted to the radiation table.* It sounds so medieval, as if someone might decide to tar and feather me before I ring the victory bell.

I think I'll be okay, I say.

After all, I have prevented myself from sneezing on the table at least three times.

Cancer requires control, I have learned.

Cancer requires a lot of control.

the hawthorne hotel, the dash

Pru, my oldest cat, pukes all over the hotel sheets on her very own queen bed. She does this at 3 a.m., and I have to toss the blankets and sheets in the bathtub to prevent staining. It appears that she has vomited at least three days of food, and I am too angry and asleep to worry about her. If I had to guess, though, I would assume she has done this out of spite.

And why do hotel linens always have to be so white?

Brown linens. Brown linens would make it so much easier to cope.

wake forest baptist hospital, office visit, the dash

You have everyone on pins and needles about this book, Dr. Stroupe tells me.

I can sense his nervousness. It is the first time in my life I have made a doctor feel uneasy instead of the other way around.

I have changed everyone's names, I say.

I have not changed anyone's name. I need to do this. This is a good reminder.

I wish I could change Dr. Stroupe's cliché, but I have no authority to do so. I want to make this book breathable, relatable.

People speak in clichés.

Just make the nurses look good, he says.

I want to make everyone *look good* in this book, I think. The doctors here at Wake Forest Baptist—or *The Big Baptist House,* as my radie ladies call it—have all been so kind and lovely and caring. The doctors have spent an adequate amount of time answering my questions and meeting my needs and allowing me to feel cared for, despite the dismal diagnosis.

I have nothing bad to say, nothing negative to write.

Although I do need to change the names.

This seems like a requirement, no matter what.

I wish I could tell Dr. Stroupe what Jon—Dr. Lucas—told me.

If I was going through this or Veronica was going through this, I would want Dr. Stroupe on my team. He is phenomenal. He is the one I would want to treat either of us.

Of course, I do not tell Dr. Stroupe this, but maybe he will read it someday in this book. Who knows?

I know nothing.

So what is the purpose in writing this book? Dr. Stroupe asks.

This is what I mean—he cares. He really, truly cares about his patients. He does not have to ask me about this book; he does not have to ask me anything except how my chemo pills are doing and if I am having any side effects from ingesting the white Temodar capsules each day. This is all that is required of him, yet he wants to know about my book.

The purpose of writing.

My reason, my why.

My first creative writing instructor in college would ask us this: *What is the purpose? If you can't answer that question, then you need to rethink your story.*

I surprise myself with the answer.

It's a narrative of what happens when the unexpected wrecks your life. I hope that when people read it, they can face whatever they are going through.

But this information is misleading, at least a tad.

This was never meant to be an uplifting, inspiring tale. We all, including Dr. Stroupe, know how it will end. I am going to die, at least in a few years, and perhaps no one will even read this book. It will exist just to exist, and that is all I require of what I have done.

To exist.

Its purpose is to exist.

Not to inspire, not to help, not to *make things okay.* I cannot *make things okay* for myself or for anyone else. I can just observe and record, an entity watching myself and my body go through these tests, these procedures, these emotions.

I really like your hat and your sweater, Dr. Stroupe tells me. Is he sucking up so he appears likable in the book? He does not have to do this. I hope I have made him seem likable, because he certainly is.

Well, even though I'm nervous, I think it's great you are writing this book. I don't think I've ever had a patient write a book before. How many words do you have?

I have trained him to ask about word count instead of pages. People always want to know pages, but I have single spaced everything on a page size quite different from that of a book.

Almost 55,000 words, I say.

And how many pages is that?

Some habits, like smoking cigarettes, are hard to break.

Um, maybe 200? I answer.

I have no idea.

Wow, that's a lot. And how long have you been working on this?

55 days, I answer. *I write 1000 words per day. It keeps me going.*

So you started this…when?

When I was in the Sticht Center, I say. *As soon as I got my computer back, I knew I had to write about this. It was inside of me, ready to burst out. Just like that stupid tumor.*

Remind me how you've set it all up?

The first section is about the seizure, the diagnosis, and the surgery. Then, the recovery. The last part is about the treatment and learning to cope with what's happening to me.

People can read it and it will help them, he says.

Well, I'm not sure about that, I say.

But it will certainly help me. It already has.

You know, I say. *I always wanted to get paid for writing. Getting a full semester off but still receiving a paycheck has allowed me to write without losing any money or time.*

You certainly are a glass-half-full type person, aren't you? he says.

I have never seen myself this way. In fact, I have always seen myself as a realist, if not a negative person. I have never thought of negativity as a *bad thing*, as something that *needs to be fixed*. Negativity is just a different way of viewing the present, a realistic method of determining what needs to happen next.

Perhaps that does make me a *glass-half-full person*.

Just promise you'll make my nurses look good, he says.

I will, Dr. Stroupe. I promise I will.

wake forest baptist hospital, comprehensive cancer center, the dash

I like my kind, sweet radiation friend.

She is a sister, though she waits for her relative in the hallway instead of at the Shell gas station like my own. I do not mind that Sarah does this; I find it rather endearing. Sarah comes to pick me up with stories regaling nurses who smoke (and want to hide the truth from their patients) and people who hold a cigarette in one hand and their IV pole in the other. We are still unsure why these people (who often look like children) are allowed to leave the hospital with their IVs and smoke cigs at the Shell station, but they do so in groups of three or more, which makes it seem okay.

My friend knows my name, but she removes the *Z*.

Sue Ann.

I correct her, but I do not mind *Sue Ann* as much as *Susan*. There is a one-letter difference instead of a three-letter difference, and in my shitty brain, this matters.

I do not think we have introduced ourselves—I assume she knows my name because the radie ladies say *SZ* once they finish with her sister. If my friend has told me her name, I have forgotten. I once had a memory like a rabbit trap, but now their feet kick and slide out before names and places and people form on my tongue.

Her sister receives her chemotherapy somewhere else, and I cannot pronounce the name of the town. It ends in *ons*. I know that much. I cannot pronounce the name of the town because I cannot tell what my new friend says. She speaks so quickly and I am so tired and there is so much going on.

Sometimes my friend talks on the phone while she waits.

This always makes me slightly sad.

Just as most patients in the Sticht Center did not discuss their diagnosis or what happened to them, I do not ask what type of cancer my friend's sister has. I know she takes chemo intravenously, so I assume she does not have brain cancer.

I am lucky, so lucky that I do not have to take chemo intravenously. I do not understand why everyone cannot take a simple pill, cannot wake up in the morning and swallow their chemo down with some Coke or orange juice, and then go about their day. Instead, some (like my friend's sister and maybe the people absconding to the Shell station for their cigarettes) have to sit for hours attached to wires and wait for the medicine to kill their cancer cells and maybe their souls.

This is not fair.

Nothing regarding cancer is fair.

Thank Jesus I'm retired, my friend says as she hangs up her cell phone. *If I wasn't retired, then I don't know who would have brought my sister to these treatments. No one could have. I mean, no one expects cancer to happen, but it happened at the right time for us.*

People and families affected by cancer speak in these altruisms. *It happened at the right time.*

If I wasn't x, then y.

If this would have happened to me in the middle of a semester, I don't know what I would have done. I might not have been able to find anyone to take over my classes. I might not have gotten my grades turned in.

I remember turning in my final three student grades before meeting Feeney, before she had to place me on the floor of the coffee shop while my right leg shook with unwanted electricity. What if I hadn't turned in any grades yet? What if I had already started a new semester? What if I had already met my students, given them a syllabus, and told them what to expect for their first assignment?

This could have been more difficult.

What if my own sister did not have a boss whose brother also had a brain tumor? What if her friend could not have rushed from Salt Lake City to New York City to take Sarah's spot in the salon for a month?

So many maybes; so many what-ifs.

We have to thank Jesus for answering the maybes, my friend says. *We have to give praise for the what-ifs that never happened.*

I am not sure I completely agree, but I smile as they release her sister and call my name, the z included.

boone, north carolina

Colleagues I have never met—after all, the English department is reportedly the biggest on campus—take my trash to the dump for me. They pick up my mail. They keep asking what food I need, but I do not require anything. I am barely eating anything except an occasional sip of the bone broth Feeney brought to my hotel room. I read on the internet that a few people with brain cancer, specifically glioblastomas, die from anorexia. What a way to go, I think. I've been simultaneously muscular and chubby my entire life—anorexia has never been a concern, though I did write about Victorian-era males with anorexia in my dissertation.

I hated my dissertation.

It had potential. Potential I never reached. But oh well.

These colleagues show me kindness. Goodness. Patience.

They perform the menial tasks I cannot handle.

They are the most supportive department on campus.

the hawthorne hotel, the dash

I fall when I get cocky and try to put on my shoes standing up. I get the left shoe on without trouble, but I lose my balance when I try to slip the right sneaker on my foot. I crash into the hotel dresser. My shoulder slams into the drawer handles like it once did to opposing jammers on the roller derby track.

Everything hurts.

Help.

I've fallen! And I can't get up!

I still do not regret refusing to get a Life Alert button or necklace. My nana died with hers around her neck like an ivory cross waiting for Jesus.

Help. I've fallen. And I can't get up!

But I do get up. I roll to my side, just as Bentley taught me in physical therapy. I place the knee closest to the dresser up first, and then I prop my hand near the television.

I am unready. Willing, but unready. My shoulder pulses, and I know there will be a bruise.

I steady myself by attempting to balance on one knee. Good. Ready. I pull myself up and notice my shoe has fallen completely off.

I was going to go for a walk, but it is dark now.

I put on the shoe again and go anyway.

I forget to wear my headdress.

The sun has nearly set but provides a golden glow for my quick evening stroll. I notice the flatness of the horizon here; I never see sunsets in Boone because I live in the middle of a mountain.

I meet a couple walking a granddog named Gracie. Gracie already has on her red-and-white polka-dotted pajamas and is ready for bed once they get home. Gracie hugs my leg—much like JC's dog Miriam does—and the couple asks why I am here. I forget that I have nothing on my head, so I do not feel self-conscious, not yet. I tell them *I have cancer and am receiving treatments at the Big Baptist House*, and they laugh.

I continue my walk.

Everyone says hello, hi, how are you?

Here in Winston-Salem, here in The Dash, I watch planes take off and shoot toward the moon. I count four as I walk, although one looks more like a rocket than a plane. I want to be on that rocket; I want to be on that plane.

As I finish the quick stroll, I see a mother and her little girl getting ready to check in to The Hawthorne. They appear to be on vacation, but one never knows. I expect the little girl to stare at my half-bald head, but she plays with a stuffed puppy dog and speaks in childish gibberish that only her mother understands.

Neither one of them notices me, and I am thankful.

I am thankful for so many things.

wake forest baptist hospital, comprehensive cancer center, the dash

If I stare at the red numbers on the ceiling they will go away.

If I stare at the red numbers on the ceiling they will go away.

If I stare at the red numbers on the ceiling I will go away.

the dash

I have so many Uber drivers thinking of me and praying for me.

Thoughts and prayers thoughts and prayers thoughts and prayers.

the hawthorne hotel, the dash

Alex and I have been texting more.

Who knows what will come of this.

I do not know why I like Alex. We have very little in common. She plays bass for musical theater. I'm an English teacher (former English teacher?) and a writer.

I am dying.

I suppose a little of Alex is dying as well.

Maybe this is why we connect.

But we don't always talk about this.

Sometimes we discuss stupid shit.

Like Mario Kart.

Alex believes she can beat me. One morning, she makes multiple graphs and charts in attempt to prove this.

I do not know if I have ever made a graph or a chart outside of my last math class my freshman year of college.

I poll my cats, and both agree that I would take Alex down in a game of Mario Kart.

I believe them.

the hawthorne hotel, the dash

Dear Number One:

I wonder about you. You do not know me, but I lived in room #301 before you arrived. Any of you. All of you. I am sure at this point, you have discovered that they call you Number One. This seems impersonal, but it's easier than a name and does not break any privacy laws. They can say *Number One needs to use the bathroom*, and no one can bitch or complain.

So there's that.

What do you think of the life flights? Did they tell you that *it's mostly organ donations*? That's a lie. If you are lucky enough to stand, if you are lucky enough to walk around, then you will realize that dying people, sick people, wrecked people, tragic people come through those back helicopter doors all the time.

Speaking of walking, how is that going? I hope you are killing it. I hope you are up and out of a wheelchair within the week. You will think that maybe you will not walk again, but Bentley or Someone New will work with you in physical therapy so you can start to live your life again. You'll find yourself between those parallel bars and doubt every slight movement, every half-an-inch. If you are anything like me, any of you,

SUZANNE SAMPLES

you will remember being a kid and excelling at gymnastics. You will look at those bars and remember flipping over them with ease. They were instruments, but now they are props. Necessary assistants for the most basic human activity: walking.

I hope you are standing up straight. I had trouble with this. I did not want to look forward because I was afraid. Because I was scared. Because I was terrified that I would never walk like a normal person again. I played roller derby, goddammit. I was a national champion baton twirler. I did not think I needed to learn to walk again. But I did. Oh, how I did. I had to start from the beginning, like a baby. Instead of gliding around a rink on a pair of quad-wheeled roller skates, I was dragging my right leg behind me like a child's blanket. I was afraid. I was so afraid. I was so, so afraid. Later, one of my doctors told me he was surprised I walked again. He did not think I would, but he did not want to tell me this.

I am glad he did not.

One day, walking started to click. Funny enough, it was after one of my physical therapists took away all assistive devices except for my foot brace. The foot brace, if you remember, pulled my foot toward the ceiling to prevent the dragging. Once he took away the walker, once he took away the wheelchair, I started to walk normally again.

I cried.

Oh how I cried.

I'm sorry, I said. *It's just the first time I have cried…about this particular thing.* .

On that day, I did not have Bentley, my regular therapist, with me. Instead, I had a different guy who did not really acknowledge my emotions.

Later he did, though.

Later he did.

The other day you got a little emotional when you walked without your walker and did not use a wheelchair, he said. *So you don't need that shit. You can go without it.*

I admired him after that. I think his name was Rob, but the chemo is fucking with my brain. I keep forgetting things I should remember.

How are Becky and Linda? They were my favorite nurses. They were a good team. They kept my blood sugar where it should have been and never chided me for trying things on my own. Becky is the one who taught me to put in a tampon with my left hand and helped me clean myself up when there was blood all over my palm. When I finally stood up and started walking on my own, I could not believe how small Linda was. She is a good two inches shorter than I am, and I am really fucking short.

I simultaneously hope you are old and hope you are young. I hope you are old because a young person—someone under 40, anyway—should never have to go through something like this. It is absolute hell. It is the worst thing that could ever happen to you. It is awful. It is shit. It is horrific. However, if you are young, you will change. You will stop taking daily activities (like taking a shower, washing your hair, brushing your teeth, and taking a shit) for granted. You will learn to appreciate sunrises and eating breakfast at 7 a.m. You will talk to older people and learn how difficult life can be over 50. One day you will miss that feta omelet you ate every morning because the steroids made you feel as if you were so hungry you could eat the tile off the bathroom floor.

But I also hope you are old. I hope you are old because older people expect this sort of thing to happen. When you get older, you expect strokes. You expect cancers. You expect *bad shit to go down*. You may not know what kind of bad shit, but you know it is coming. You prepare. You write wills. You create advanced directives. You get ready.

If you are young, you are not ready.

I wonder if you had surgery. You probably did. Whether you had a stroke or a tumor, you likely have staples or a scar of some sort. We all did. Sometimes at breakfast, I would try to count the staples on other peoples' heads. I would often get bored or distracted around the teens. I'm sure you've learned how you don't really ask what happened to people. You stay quiet. You assume things. You might have one or two who are *willing to talk*, but for the most part, people just go about their business of rehabilitating and do not speak of the past.

Sometimes I wonder.

I wonder about Cheleda, who said she was going to write a book once she left. I'll be honest—I did not believe her. She refused to sit up in her wheelchair for the nurses, she would not eat, and she would not leave her wheelchair and attempt to walk. She was stubborn and expressed discontent toward everything. I saw her in the hospital elevator the other day. She looked good, much better than she did when she was my near neighbor, but she was still in the wheelchair and did not look motivated to write a book.

I wonder about Papaw who wore his matching pajama tops and bottoms to breakfast every morning. The same Papaw who actually did ask me why I was there and then proceeded to tell me about how he did not know he had a brain tumor until he *almost cut the danged thing out himself* when he flipped over his lawnmower. He liked that I played roller derby and hoped I would be back on skates before too long.

I still haven't been back on skates, but sometimes I wonder if skating might be easier than walking. Wheels are never a bad thing, right? I also cannot drive, but perhaps skates would allow me to maneuver around town a bit easier. I could, at the very least, roll down the street.

But anyway, this is about you. I hope you have faith of some sort. If not in a higher power, then in yourself. At the end of the day, you are all you have. I hope you have strength. I hope you have a strong will.

Otherwise, let's be honest, you are fucked.

So fucked.

Pardon my language?

Eh, fuck it. I hope you have motherfucking strength.

Patient Number One: you will need motherfucking strength and a goddamn strong will.

You will need it.

Sincerely,

Former Patient Number One

nowhere

I remember visiting my sister in Brooklyn last summer. I was dating Chole and missed her because we were in a new relationship, and I didn't know her well enough yet. When my trip ended before it should have, Chole refused to pick me up at the airport with my car I lent her because she had scheduled a movie date with a friend *and didn't want to cancel on her.*

Chole was angry I came back early because she said she *needed space* from me. We had only been dating two months, and I did not understand. Chole did not have her own car or a valid driver's license (although she said she did so she could have my car for two weeks), so we only saw each other about once a week. Since my 30s, I'd never dated someone who only wanted to see me once a week.

I'm independent, Chole told me through a text.

I was sitting on the airport floor, crying.

No, you're not, bitch, you have a roommate and a trust fund and friends around you 24 hours a day. They sleep in your bed and on your couch. You are the opposite of independent.

That's fine, I say. *I understand. I'll just Uber to your house so I can get my car and my dog.*

I should have known then.

Sarah and I had plans in Brooklyn. She showed me the belly of the city. We never went to Times Square, though I did make her take me to see the Statue of Liberty.

The Night Everything Went Wrong, I ended up on the train with a drag queen who told me *family should not treat you like that.*

The drag queen texted me the next day to ensure I was okay. People in New York were way friendlier than I ever imagined.

Sarah and I ended the night in a karaoke bar with her friend Jimmy More Cowbell Lafavor. That is not his real name. I do not know Jimmy's real name. All I know is that my sister met him on a Tinder date in Asheville, and he was always around and always kinda weird and always willing to meet up and drink.

We thought he might be gay.

I tried to tease this information from him so we would know if he was hitting on my sister or just trying to be friends.

This is important when people like Jimmy start acting a little bit creepy.

We walked down Avenue B. We are only slightly drunk at this point. I had no idea.

Chole wasn't responding to my last text, but I didn't care. She was probably drunk on the porch with their friends.

No big deal.

She was actually sexting her ex-girlfriend.

No big deal.

I kicked rocks down Avenue B as I questioned Jimmy More Cowbell Lafavor with the intensity of a prosecuting attorney.

So…are you seeing anyone?

Anybody?

Any girls?

Guys?

People?

Jimmy gets quiet. I typically would not pressure anyone to spill the secrets of their personal life, but here we were with Jimmy in the dark, and I would never let my sister go back to his hotel room with him if he answered *I'm straight and single* or *I'm straight and with a girl but don't care.*

Poor Jimmy.

He could never win.

As I kick more rocks and prosecute Jimmy More Cowbell Lafavor, I have no idea that Chole is sexting her ex-girlfriend. I have no idea that I have a fucking brain tumor. I have no clue that in a few months, I will require a craniotomy, chemotherapy, and daily radiation treatments.

The rocks and I know nothing about this.

We find ourselves at a karaoke bar. It must be one in the morning already, but we don't care. My sister keeps demanding to see the *secret heavy metal karaoke list*, but no one acquiesces.

I am tired.

I am fussy.

Chole never responded to my *I love you* text.

I should have known then.

I am ready to leave.

I want you to sing with me, this guy in his 50s says to me. He sits beside me on the barstool. There is too much pink, too much fuzz, for me to feel comfortable here.

He hands me a purple microphone.

There is too much zebra print.

The Sheryl Crow and Kid Rock song begins.

I have no choice.

The dude winks at me and grabs my hand as he sings. I play along. I might as well try to have fun.

This will be my final chance.

Sarah and Jimmy More Cowbell Lafavor disappear.

I panic and grab my sister's backpack. I walk out of the bar and search for her on the street. I do not see her cotton-candy-pink hair anywhere.

And then I meet the drag queen.

I call Sarah and hear the bag buzz.

Chole has not yet responded to my text.

I should have known then.

My head does not hurt. Nothing hurts yet. Nothing moves. Nothing twitches. I have no reason to worry, not yet.

I head toward the train. Sarah and Jimmy likely ditched me and already hopped on, I think. Or maybe they found a secret karaoke room with the secret heavy metal karaoke song list.

The possibilities are endless.

I remember everything.

I remember how to get back to my sister's basement apartment. I make no mistakes. No missteps. I have a horrible sense of direction, but I use landmarks and maps and my brain. Nothing seems wrong.

Nothing seems wrong at all.

My sister returns four hours later. She has no phone, no metro card, and no way of contacting anyone. Although I assumed she was with Jimmy, she is alone. Her boyfriend, Gio, who, with his wide grin, resembles a Puerto Rican Steve Harvey, waits for her by sleeping on the couch.

She had a tougher time than I did.

She is fucking wasted.

She is not happy about any of this.

Where the fuck were you? she screams at me. *Where. The. Fuck?*

I lost you, I stammer.

Obviously.

Gio awakes and turns white. He is afraid of her; so am I.

You think you are really something, she says. *You think you can just walk around this city and somehow be okay. What the fuck is wrong with you? You think because you went to Ph.D. school that you are better than everyone? Pack your shit. Get out of here. Get the fuck out of my apartment.*

So I do.

But she won't leave me alone. As I *pack my shit,* Sarah follows me around her basement, throwing her hands in my face and like an irritating cat, sliding what I need to pack off the surfaces and tables.

Ph.D. school Ph.D. school Ph.D. school.

I slap her.

She falls asleep.

I request an Uber and begin texting Chole.

Wake up. Please wake up. I'm coming home.

No one cares.

I wonder now. I wonder now if there was something wrong with me then. If the tumor had started to form, and I just had no idea. Not yet. Was I acting? Was I reacting? I am still not sure. Technically, I did nothing wrong. I lost Sarah and assumed she ran away with Jimmy Whatshisface Whatadouchehat.

Jimmy gets married three months later. To a girl we have never heard him mention.

Typical.

I cannot change my plane ticket, so I buy a new one. This feels wrong, frivolous. I could have waited for Sarah to cool down; I could have waited for everything to blow over. I could have stayed longer, stuck with the original plan.

But I wanted to make a point; I wanted to prove I was okay.

Days before this: *You seem off. Are you okay?*

My blood sugar is low. People seem off when they have a low blood sugar. You should know this by now.

But maybe there was something else, something even more sinister that none of us knew about yet.

Chole refuses to pick me up. The friend date. She can't cancel. She has my car.

Fuck all of them.

I Uber from Charlotte to Asheville so I can get my car and my dog.

Chole is angry that I am back early. She still needs *fucking space*. Sarah is angry that I left early. She did not want fucking space.

I had a brain tumor the whole time, probably. Maybe. Hard to say.

The only person really worried about me is my new drag queen friend. She texts me when I return to Asheville.

You okay? she asks.

I think so, I say, but I have no idea what is about to come.

the hawthorne hotel, the dash

Prufrock paces in her cage like a hungry tigress. I have to keep her crated in the hotel when I leave for treatments. Will she eat me when I die, I wonder? Will she tear apart my ligaments until there is nothing of me left? She mews. She walks. She waits.

the hawthorne hotel, the dash

I read how having elevated glucose levels and type one diabetes *serves as great prevention against brain cancers*. Sure, this is not a peer-reviewed article, and I am an academic and therefore, I should know better, but I can't help but note the ethos of the writing.

Based on a study at Ohio State…

No peer review on this article, but it seems the writers at least reference a peer-reviewed article.

Higher blood glucose levels have been shown to prevent gliomas in patients.

This is the greatest irony of my life.

I've spent 31 years dealing with type one diabetes, and let's be honest, no one fucking gets it. Most people think diabetes is what happens when you are old, fat, and unhealthy. That is type two diabetes, and some with type two diabetes are actually a healthy weight.

Type one, though?

Type one is autoimmune and drains the life out of your muscles, skin, and bone.

Type one is a needle jab to the gut four times a day, a life spent waiting to die.

Brain cancer?

Brain cancer is a quick bullet that requires immediate life support.

Type one takes more time.

They both still suck, and dealing with them simultaneously will be the death of me.

Of course, this isn't fair.

Of course, no one wants this for me.

Of course, no one wished this on me, although Chole might have because she is a giant, infected cunt, and she only cares about herself and her new girlfriend, who is still in her early 20s and thinks *being queer* is enough of an identity to survive.

Patients with elevated blood glucose levels do not frequently experience brain cancers as much as those with normalized blood glucose levels.

I want to make it. I desire to live. I yearn to beat these fucking diseases and prove myself beyond anything that has sought to define my health or my being.

I want to be a badass.

Happy International Women's Day!

I want to be better than everyone thinks I am.

I don't feel sick I don't feel sick I don't feel sick.

on the way to CVS, the dash

A homeless man asks me for 23 cents. *I'm just trying to survive, man. I'm just trying to make it,* I tell him. I do not give him any money. Five months ago, I would have. But now, now I just have nothing left to give.

the dash

There are so many Uber drivers in Winston-Salem, North
    Carolina, praying for me.

comprehensive cancer center, the dash

Debbie, my favorite radie lady, loves playing 80s music on Fridays. Most days, she plays Celine Dion or some other form of digestible noise that burns my ears as much as the radiation scorches my brain.

But Fridays?

Fridays are Foreigner.

the hawthorne hotel, the dash

Alex asks me to trade a dark secret.

I tell her about the time I walked in on my grandfather watching porn and jacking off. I was 11; I had never seen a naked female body other than my own. The lady was on a stage with a man deep in her pussy.

I froze.

I could not move.

Eventually, I turned and ran back to the yard.

I have never told anyone until now.

I have only met Alex once.

I will not reveal Alex's secret here.

It is not mine to tell.

the hawthorne hotel, the dash

All I want to eat are Red Delicious apples. I could consume a bag a day. Thinking of chewing anything else makes me nauseous, makes me want to vomit all over the pristinely white hotel bathroom where I will spend the next two weeks wishing for my health.

nowhere

I haven't heard from JC all day. I'm not sure what's going on with her. Does she know about Alex? Does she know about my new friendship? Does she feel completely shut out of my brain like that fucking tumor?

wake forest baptist hospital, comprehensive cancer center, the dash

There is an ovular pattern of hair loss on my scalp. From one side to the next. The radie ladies gently tease me. *We really gave you a nice haircut, didn't we?* I laugh. What else can I do? The lines on my head are precisely drawn. I am ugly. I have no idea who I am anymore.

nowhere

Dear Leftover Tumor Parts/Branches/Cells:

I do not know if you still exist. One of my doctors says that we *must do another MRI, but we can't do it too soon. Otherwise, a bunch of swelling from the radiation will just show up. It will be impossible to tell.*

You and I have not spoken for quite some time, tumor.

I have not written to you.

I have not written about you.

I have not forgotten, though.

I have not forgotten how you started this whole mess, this whole ordeal.

I did not realize, not at first, that I was never alone. You were with me at least a month before I had the seizure in the coffee shop. I would go to bed at night and mourn my loneliness, but you were right beside me the entire time. If I had known this, if I had been aware, I would have spoken to you more gently so you might have been nicer to me by the time you fucked everything up. I would have spoken to you sweetly, whispered your name, stroked my head before I fell asleep.

But I was too blind to realize you existed.

I was too stubborn.

I was too interested in other aspects of my life.

Now you aren't there, but as the doctors have explained, this does not mean you are gone.

You might have tentacles, little octopi cells that had already spread throughout my brain before the surgeon could remove them. That is the point of all this chemo, all this radiation. To get rid of you for good. But that is never a guarantee, my medical team explains to me. There is never a promise you are gone forever.

The doctor in charge of my radiation, Dr. Crowder, speaks to me like a friend. *There are other things we can try if the tumor comes back. But if your scan looks good, then we can stretch out the times we see you. I know you're coming from far away, so we do not want you driving here more than you have to.*

I imagine she is telling me about a restaurant. *There are other things you can try if you do not like the lasagna. If it doesn't agree with you, the menu has so many other options that might better suit you. If you're feeling up to it, we can try some of those. But I know you're driving from a place out-of-town, so I do not want you coming back if you just don't feel up to it.*

But she's not talking to me about a restaurant; she is talking to me about my health, my existence, my being.

We don't want you coming back because we want you to be healthy.

We have to keep a really close eye on GBMs, though, she says.

In translation: you will be back here all the time because this cancer is going to fucking kill you. The lasagna is going to eat you. You are dead. We are just prolonging your time here on earth.

Thank you, tumor.

This is where you have brought me, to one of the best neuro-surgery centers in the nation.

the dash

Sometimes all of this nonsense makes me think of my father.

The Michael Martin Murphey single "Carolina in the Pines" the day of my birth.

How could he have known? How could he have known I would die in Carolina? How could he have known that brain cancer would have brought me here to face my end? How did he know that his musical leanings would inspire me to stay away from the mainstream and only listen to indie bands until the final chapter of my life? How did he know he would love me so much, so fiercely, that he refused to believe I had cancer at all and didn't call because he thought I was okay and *didn't want to bother me?*

I have always been close with my father.

We do not need phone calls.

I have my mother for that.

A different kind of closeness.

For you, brain cancer, I have nothing but hatred. I cannot feel indifferent toward you because you are inside me. You are part of me. You are there, and I didn't even know at first. I can only hate you because I know you so well. I can only despise you because you latched onto my frontal lobe and like a small child with its mother, refused to let me go.

I did not really say goodbye to the main tumor, but I did mourn.

It was a piece of me, after all.

the road, the dash

Do you have a family? my Uber driver asks me.

Of course I have a family, moron. Most people have some sort of family, even if it's a nontraditional one.

Yes, I have two parents and a sister who care a lot about me. And many friends. I am lucky.

No, I mean, do you have a husband? Kids of your own?

I do not like the way he asks me this question. It is as if a husband and kids would make this experience harder, more difficult for me. It is as if I had kids of my own, there would be more suffering and more hurt and more pain than I already have.

No, I do not, I say.

It's a good thing you don't have kids, the driver says. *Would just make it harder for everyone, you know?*

I do not answer. I think this was a question? From living in the South for many years now, I have learned there are no private moments. Sure, people are friendly, but they want to know everything about you. Who you are. What choices you have made. Your religious preferences.

I mean, kids, wow, can you imagine trying to tell your kids you have brain cancer?

Can you imagine trying to tell your father you have brain cancer? I made my mom do it. Can you imagine trying to tell your sister you have brain cancer? I made my mom do that, too. It's not easy to tell anyone you love that you have brain cancer. It does not matter how old they are, their status as friends or family, or anything else.

It is hard, and it fucking sucks.

Yeah, thank god I never had them, I say. *Stupid little shits would have made it difficult for me to do whatever I love the most in the last few minutes of my life.*

I see that you lost your hair. Cancer got it, I suppose.

This guy does not quit. I miss Uber drivers who listen to the radio and do not want to have a conversation about my personal life.

Yep. Got almost all of it.

Thank god I didn't have kids thank god I didn't have kids thank god I didn't have kids.

So do you regret…

We pull into the Hawthorne, but he does not drive to the door. He parks the car about four feet past the door. Fuck, I think, I'm going to die. Sooner than I thought. Faster than I thought. Those 12 to 15 months just dwindled down to a few seconds.

Look, I don't want to creep you out or anything.

Too late, buddy. Too late.

He lifts a planner from the console. The planner is from 2015.

If you don't mind, give me your email, and I'll pass it along to my senior pastor. I'm actually meeting up with him for lunch later today. Have you felt like eating lately?

No.

No, I have not felt like eating lately, especially with old dudes who use religion to mask creepiness.

I make up an email and write something down.

If you don't mind, I'd like to pray for you.

I think I'll just—

And then I remember—I am in a van where the driver has to open the door.

Dear God, Please place your hands on this young woman and protect her from the harm the world has thrust upon her.

I keep my eyes open and watch this loser through the rearview mirror. I am close enough to the hotel that I could scream and someone might hear me.

I decide to wait for the *amen* and leave peacefully. I do not doubt, not really, that this driver will let me leave the van. He just wants to push his personal brand of Christianity on me because that's what he feels like he must do.

She did nothing to deserve this terrible cancer, but here she is. Here she is in your arms now, asking for forgiveness and allowing you to take charge of her life.

I did not agree to this I did not agree to this I did not agree to this.

We ask that you to take over where she has faltered. Where others weaker than you have faltered.

In Jesus' name we pray, I interject. *Amen.*

I wish you the best, he says as he finally opens the door.

One star. Zero stars. Negative stars.

I try to eject myself from the van quickly, but my right side is still weak. Getting out of vehicles is still one of my most difficult activities.

I'll continue praying for you and email you about lunch, the driver says.

I do not feel sick I do not feel sick I do not feel sick.

I feel sick.

Sick of this type of shit. Sick of explaining to people why I wear a rag over my head and have lost my hair. Why I have trouble getting comfortable because of my right side. Why I can't sleep at night. Why I do not feel like eating. Why I am not working. Why I am taking an Uber to and from the Comprehensive Cancer Center every single day. Why why why. Why I get stuck in these vehicles explaining to random drivers why having cancer must be easy because I never had children.

This must make it easier, right?

People are always looking for ways to justify the wrongs of the world.

It's a good thing I never had children; cancer would be impossible to explain to them, you know?

Please pray for me.

nowhere

I have this memory of my sister before she left Boone: *one day I woke up and felt really awful about myself. I put concealer all over my face and had the best day ever.*

the hawthorne hotel, the dash

The Mystery of Bobbi Adolf!

I have three days left of radiation.

Bored one night, I scroll through my text messages. Since getting the iPhone X, I have no longer needed to delete every message on my phone after three days. I got the phone with *mega memory*, so now I can keep everything forever.

I can keep everything longer than myself.

I find a string of texts from right after my surgery.

The number is a WV area code; since this is where I am from, I must know these people. They sent texts of a black and white furry cat with a child holding the animal. I do not recognize the animal or the child. The cat is extra fluffy and has a black mustache.

The cat lacks a tail.

We call her Bobbi Adolf, one text reads.

I have no memory of any of this.

Bobbi=bobtail.

Adolf=mustache.

This is the most WV thing I have seen in months.

I adore my home state, but sometimes. Sometimes. Sometimes. Wow. Sometimes, people do not think before they name their cats.

She adopted us, the next text reads. *We just love her to death.*

Good old Bobbi Adolf.

There is also a WV blanket in the texts, so I assume my mother must know these people. I text her to find out.

Do you know who these people are? I ask as I send the accompanying picture of the child holding the cat.

No, she responds. *Did you ask them?*

No, I write. *They texted me after my surgery, and I never responded.*

Ask them, she says.

Of course, that would be the easiest thing. But now it's three months post-surgery and post-text, and it's too late to ask them. They told me about Bobbi Adolf with such familiarity that my mom *must* know them. There is no other explanation.

Who is Bobbi Adolf?

The world needs to know.

That's the only way to find out, my mom says.

Cancer makes everyone familiar with you. It does not matter if you do not remember them or know them or have even spoken to them; the disease makes everyone your loved one, everyone your friend, everyone your family.

Even cats named Bobbi Adolf.

I wonder about Bobbi Adolf. Who is she? Does she come inside at night? Does she go outside at all? Bobbi Adolf is so fluffy and pretty that I hope she stays inside all day and watches rainbows and caterpillars and drops of water fade slowly down the kitchen windows.

Oh, Bobbi Adolf.

I do not respond to the text or ask who they are. It is far too late to know about Bobbi Adolf; it is far too late to question the people who might care about me the most.

#whoisbobbiadolf

the hawthorne hotel, the dash

I wake up to a barrage of text messages from a friend who claims they are in love with me.

This has happened more than once since my diagnosis. Men, women, people I never thought of in any way except as friends. But they showed up and here I am dying and everyone is suddenly in love with me.

Maybe it is easier than I thought to love the dying, to connect.

I do not think anyone loved me when I was actually living.

It is hard to say. Hard to tell. Hard to decipher.

How do I know what love is real? How can I tell? How can I be sure?

I don't know how to say this, the text reads, *but I was in love with you from the minute I saw you. your smile did something to me. tore me up inside. everyone else looked the same but you were different. there was something about you. i didn't want either of us to die without me saying something. you don't have to respond but i just wanted you to know.*

I put down my phone and hope I remember to deal with this later.

nowhere

I keep dreaming of the past, but different outcomes occur.

For example: I am with my sister and her perfectly permed blonde hair. She is four, and I am seven. I know I am about to burn her with a curling iron. I have the iron in my hand and realize the power it wields. I have considered this memory many times in adulthood. Why did I burn her? It was just a slight scorch, a little mark, sure, but it was mean. It was cruel. It was not something a protective big sister should ever do, but I did it anyway.

We had seen our mother use this curling iron, the same one, on her bangs daily. We would both sit and watch her *make herself look pretty* with this tool, and we admired her beauty from the bathroom mirror. All three of our reflections wondered how she became so gorgeous and how our quiet, gentle father convinced such a, sassy fireball to go on a single date with him.

But now I have the iron. In my tiny hand. Ready to burn the jealousy out of my sister's porcelain doll skin.

We all know what happens next.

Except that it doesn't.

This time has changed; this time is different.

I put down the curling iron and help flop her hair into the perfect 80s side ponytail.

the hawthorne hotel, the dash

Everything comes in waves. The tiredness. The nausea. The worry about whether or not my tumor has started to regrow. Sometimes I worry. Sometimes I feel too sick to worry. Sometimes I sit on hotel beds and write until my veins feel as dry as my brain after a microwaving session.

That's pretty much what happens, right?

I look like an egg.

I used clippers to buzz off most of my hair, and then I convince Jenna to shave the remainder off with a razor.

I sit on the toilet and let her work the razor around the most tender parts of my ears.

How was practice? I ask.

I miss derby so much.

It was...good. Tutu hurt her ankle. I think she'll be okay, though. She has to be.

I wish Jenna had more to say about derby and practice and falling and ankles. I want to discuss things that don't have the word cancer, chemo, or radiation in them. I want to hear about everything else.

I still cannot sleep at night, no matter how many or what type of pills I take.

Everything is as uncomfortable as resting on a splintered floor.

No one discusses how *cancer might make your right side quit working. Cancer might make it difficult—really difficult—for you to get in and out of cars. Cancer might make you lose your balance and fall in a lonely hotel room full of cat fur and hair that falls out of your head that leaves little pieces of you on the white pillowcases.*

I thought I got rid of enough hair, but I did not. I needed to shave the whale hump of my head dry. Or get Jenna to do it for me.

It's a BFF task, I tell her. I feel slightly manipulative, but this must be done by someone other than myself. I need to rid myself of all the hair. I must. I no longer have a choice.

I look like one of those magnetic lead toys where children use a doodle pen to give the guy little sideburns. That is what I look like.

Dear god.

Jenna shaves with precision and care.

I feel like I am hurting you, she says, but I am not sensitive, not like that, anyway.

You're doing a perfect job, I tell her.

I do not feel a single thing.

nowhere

Cancer should mean that the only obligations you have are to yourself.

the hawthorne hotel, the dash

I get some kind of weird, open wound on my chest.

wake forest baptist hospital, comprehensive cancer center, the dash

When I have three days of radiation remaining, snow falls in Winston-Salem. Unlike Boone, the Dash is not accustomed to snow, so the chunky flakes draw admirers from all over the hospital.

Doctors, patients, nurses, and technicians flock to the picture windows to see Christmas Part Two.

Sometimes things get wild here.

After a bit, the snow actually starts to stick.

The radie ladies panic. They were both late to arrive today, and now EVERYTHING IS BEHIND.

I sit and watch some stupid talk show I do not know the name of. It wouldn't matter if I did know the name of it. They are calling a random person and asking the person who answers what Mindy Kaling's daughter's name is.

Somehow, I know it's Katherine.

There is no good reason for me to know any of this.

Christmas Part Two, I realize, looks exactly like Christmas Part One did for me.

Here in the hospital.

Waiting, wishing, hoping.

west virginia

My mother has had enough and wants me home.

Home with her and my father.

Not my home in Boone.

Home in West-By-God-Virginia, where I grew up.

nowhere

I still have these dreams, these coming-of-age moments at night where the outcomes differ from how they did in real life.

Last night: I found my great-grandmother's quilts. Hundreds of them, which we knew existed. But then I found the awards. She won multiple blue ribbons at county fairs and various contests around the state.

None of us had any idea.

And then I went to the neighbor's house, where Dave Mullins once lived.

Dave is nine years older than I am. I had a crush on him when I was sixteen and he was twenty-five. This did not seem weird to me at the time; this seemed logical, mature. Of course, boys my age did not understand me.

I needed someone older, wiser.

Someone like Dave, who lived with his parents and worked as a dishwasher at the local pizza joint.

V. mature.

But in this dream, instead of pining after Dave Mullins, he gives me a car. The car is a jalopy, but I know it will run and take me wherever I plan to go. I jump in the car and drive the vehicle into the street.

When I look over to the passenger seat, instead of Dave, I see JC. She smiles at me, and we drive away from the nonsense, from the bullshit.

nowhere

Chris is very interested in my dreams. She would like me to take detailed records and email her those records. I knew she would want this. She is so weird, but in a great, lovable way.

the hawthorne hotel, the dash

You should take a souvenir from the hotel, Feeney texts me. *Then you should put whatever it is in your car and always drive around with it in there.*

I have no idea what she is talking about.

the hawthorne hotel, the dash

I start taking melatonin in the middle of the day so I can nap. I have never liked naps, but cancer likes naps. Cancer likes so many things that SZ does not. Naps. Healthy food. Radiation. Blood work.

So much blood work.

I still have no idea who Bobbi Adolf is.

Or her parents.

the hawthorne hotel, the dash

Hello? my mom texts.

She does this without any warning or pretense. It drives me insane.

I'm right here, I respond.

Lol, she says. Just checking on you.

Ready to go in for radiation, I say.

Two more days, and I am done.

Two more days of hellos? and I am finished.

comprehensive cancer center, the dash

I can't wait to ring the bell I can't wait to ring the bell I can't

wait to ring the bell.

nowhere

When I die, I want everyone to know that *House of Leaves* was one of my favorite books. You can learn a lot about someone by asking them about their favorite book. Mine has changed over time, but I really like *House of Leaves* and unreliable narrators a whole lot.

the road, the dash

I have encountered an Uber driver named Ray a few times now. On my next-to-last day of radiation, Ray drives me to the cancer center. A fellow West Virginian, Ray and I both have an eccentric fascination with the Hatfields and McCoys and how many people believe them to be legendary and not actual families.

They are real! Ray tells me. *My wife descended from the Hatfields. They are educated people, nowadays. They are school teachers. Doctors. Lawyers. But no one knows that.*

Just normal people. Just like me and Ray.

Ray readjusts his legs; I notice he is wearing a blue Snuggie with nothing underneath. His hairy, bare thighs nearly bring my nausea back to life.

But this is Ray.

Ray is probably just doing his laundry today and does not give a shit.

Ray does not threaten me.

Not at all.

You know, you're a beautiful young lady, Ray says. *And I think you're going to beat this.*

Ray also tells me he is a medical doctor. Or he was, before he retired and started driving for Uber.

For some reason, I believe Ray. I have no reason to; Ray is a storyteller. He's wearing a blue Snuggie and nothing else. His wife descended from one of the most outlawed families in the state of West Virginia. He might have been a doctor; he might have been a house painter. He might not even be an Uber driver.

But I believe him because I need to.

I believe him because I want to.

I believe him because maybe I am in a dream and none of this is real.

You're my favorite passenger ever, Ray tells me. *At first you were in my top three, but now you are my number one. You may not believe me, but I said a prayer for you the other night. I think you are going to be okay. You are special.*

I am certain Ray tells everyone this, but like I said, I believe him.

I have to believe in someone, in something.

You know I had prostate cancer, Ray says.

It's true—he told me this the other day.

You know I got the little tattoos so they could do the pinpoint radiation. Did you get those?

They put them on my mask, I tell him. *That way they didn't have to tattoo my face.*

Who would want to mess up that beautiful face? You know I said you were in my top three, but you've moved up to be my favorite Uber passenger. Of all time.

Thank you, Ray. Thank you.

You know my balls shrunk after radiation. I went from a rooster to a hen real fast.

Oh God.

Since Bobbi Adolf, this is the most West Virginia thing I've ever heard.

Ever.

Fuck.

I showed my doctor, and she didn't believe me at first. And then she saw my balls and was like Good God, Ray! You're right! You went straight from a rooster to a hen! *I drove that doctor crazy.*

Godspeed, Ray. May I see you again on my long journey to the end of this life, whenever that may be.

Whenever my time comes, I will be ready to go.

nowhere

I dream of Alex and Brad.

I have never met Brad.

I know Alex, kind of, and Alex knows Brad. They play music together and are the cutest platonic couple. They post prom-ish pictures on Instagram after they perform shows, and I want to squish myself in the middle of those photos and become part of what they are, part of the happiness, part of the fun.

I dream the three of us shop together in a thrift store.

The thrift store is magical. Like Russian nesting dolls, every crease has something to open and discover. Every envelope has an old letter, and every pocket contains a hidden a five-dollar bill.

Always something to dig for, always something to find.

I stumble upon a letterman jacket from the 1970s.

Before I was alive, before I was conceived.

Before I was a Michael Martin Murphey song on my dad's record player in the middle of December, one of the coldest days recorded in Dille, West Virginia.

The jacket is bright green with a gator decal on the lapel. Gold pins dot the fabric in memories of a forgotten hero now gone. This person played football. Might have been a quarterback or something just as fancy.

I dig into the pocket and find a purple corsage.

I know I must give this wrist corsage to Alex.

But I must do so through Brad.

I know this.

I find Brad paging through a photo album. The photos are from the early 1900s. One of the pictures features my grandma. leaning against a car. She drove a car, *yes she did*. She told me this once when I visited her. *Women were not supposed to drive*, she said, *but I thought* to hell with that *and did whatever I wanted. Can you believe that?*

I could believe it.

Yes I could.

I give Brad the corsage.

He knows what to do.

Brad and I search for Alex. We find her looking at jazzy dresses from the 1920s. I imagine that if Alex tried on these black, fringed silhouettes, she would easily fit into that decade.

Alex seems as if she belongs somewhere other than the present; I could see her hitting up a speakeasy and wordlessly playing the bass for a local jazz band in 1929.

I feel as if I have known Alex for much longer than a few months.

Closeness, I have realized, has no timeline.

Brad gets on one knee with the purple corsage and asks Alex to accompany him *to the next high school dance*. Alex blushes and says *why yes of course*. Brad loops the corsage around Alex's wrist, as if they will always belong together in some universe. I am in awe of the spectacle before me, yet somehow, I feel involved in this quaint exchange.

And then Brad fades into the dream like a lost earring at the thrift store.

Alex and I are now alone. We flip through the clothes on the rack. We do not speak. I feel so comfortable, so cared for, so alone together.

Alex smiles at me, and I finally feel no pain.

wake forest, comprehensive cancer center, the dash

I tremble with excitement during my final radiation treatment.

I want this to be over I want this to be over I want this to be over.

I ask to keep the mask. I do not own a gun, but I have the desire to take the mask to the shooting range and blow the plastic to pieces. I imagine those plastic pieces bursting into indistinguishable atoms until nothing remains.

wake forest baptist hospital, comprehensive cancer center, the dash

My radie ladies walk me toward the victory bell. I have waited to clang this apparatus for so fucking long. I have stared at this bell every single day and wanted nothing more than to ring the shit out of the damned thing.

I have heard other people ring the bell quietly, safely.

I grab the rope with my left hand, my new strong hand. I ring the bell softly at first, and then my other hand joins in the effort. I pull and push the victory bell rope, and the sound roars fucking loudly, wildly. I get stronger and louder each time the clapper clashes with the lip. (These are technical bell terms; I did my research.) The people in the waiting room applaud me and congratulate my effort.

This completion was harder than all the years and time I put into my Ph.D. or any other academic effort.

My mom records the entire ordeal.

When I watch the video later, I cannot believe how much weight I have lost. How bald I look.

How happy I look, despite dying.

comprehensive cancer center, office visit, the dash

You have just sailed through treatment, my radiation oncologist tells me. *I always seem to have one patient who sails through and one who really struggles. You are my rock star.*

I don't feel sick I don't feel sick I don't feel sick.

But I am, I guess. I always will be. It is not a conspiracy theory, as my sister would say. Doctors are not seeing me weekly, and I am not being treated daily just so the doctors or the nurses or the pharmacists can make money. I have seen the MRIs with my deformed ear and have observed the silly string monkey bread tumor that attempted to kill me and still might. I have experienced the seizures, the paralysis, the nausea, and the feeling of my right side being disassociated with the remainder of my body.

You have four weeks off, the doctor tells me. *You can basically do whatever you want.*

I wonder if she is telling me to party, telling me to drink. I think she might have if my mom had not been in the room. But then again, I might have been just feeling a little bit wild.

You are free to travel and do what you'd like, but here is a paper you can use to get your bloodwork done. They will send us the results, but so far, everything looks good. Your platelet count has actually gone up, which is…strange but good.

The thing about dying is that you think of all the things you want to do. You've been given a timeline and you know what you have to work with; but then, then, your body does not want to cooperate. You want to hop on a plane to Italy and explore nauseatingly cute little book stores, but you aren't quite coordinated enough to get on a plane without elbowing everyone in the face. You're not quite energetic enough to focus on a single book page, more or less thousands of different books.

I have to see another doctor before I leave the grips of the hospital for the month.

Dr. Stroupe, my chemo oncologist.

Well, I have to ask, he says, *how is the book coming along?*

I have frightened him with my progress and my ability to interpret what has happened to me, but I can tell he likes it.

I can tell he is proud.

A thousand words per day, I tell him. *It's what keeps me going.*

My mom accompanies me to the appointment.

And where are you from? Dr. Stroupe asks.

Harrisville, West Virginia, my mom says.

I like how she always includes the name of my miniscule hometown as if someone might recognize a place with more cows than people.

We have one stoplight, and we don't even need that. It's just there for looks.

Well, every town needs something, my doctor says. *My wife is from Charleston, West Virginia. She's a dermatologist here. She's the smart one.*

I still have confidence.

homes

the road

Before this whole cancer mess started, I did not communicate much with my mom. Tormented by differing political beliefs, our relationship suffered from polarities. Me=liberal as fuck. Her=conservative, yes.

But brain tumors change shit. They change everything. Sometimes for the better.

I am finally headed home for Christmas break.

I am tired but feel alive.

The snow flurries around us in my parents' new Buick. I do not know how they afforded this car, and I do not ask. I simply enjoy the smooth ride, enjoy the feeling of being free from the radiation mask and my head bolted to a moving table.

The carnival ride is over; the circus is done.

I do not feel sick I do not feel sick I do not feel sick.

the road

I feel the most comfortable in the car. I can sit up straight, my limbs feel like my own, and the snow on the pines looks like something from a painting, something from a dream, something from some sort of heaven.

I still have my smile.

west virginia

I assume that because I did not feel sick the day before, I will feel fine the next week.

I do not.

I remember the doctors telling me *your first week off radiation and chemo will be your worst week.*

I did not believe them.

I thought I knew more.

Thirty-one years of type one diabetes has made me trust myself more than I ever trust doctors. However, cancer is new. Cancer is different. Three months does not rival thirty-one years. Diabetes is a slow, drawn-out death; cancer is a quick blow.

You've lost a lot of weight, my dad says.

That's what not eating and throwing up everything will do to you, I guess.

My father and I have always been honest with one another. I suppose that it is a trait of our family. I remember him telling me one time *that's the thing about us. We don't dress anything up. If the doctor tells us that we're going to die, we tell our friends and family* Well, I have a few months left. I guess that's it. *Your mom's family is different. Everything is a big secret.*

He was right.

My grandmother had almost completed her treatment for breast cancer before I even knew she was diagnosed. She wore a blonde, coiffured wig that perfectly matched her hair.

No one knew.

Everyone knows about me.

Everyone knows.

west virginia

I can barely stand because of the nausea. I am dizzy. I have brief headaches that twinge through my brain like a bee sting.

But I am no longer bolted to a table; I am no longer confined in a machine that I hope will save my life.

Yet there is no way to tell.

Like the universe surrounding us, there is so much unknown.

west virginia

The texts, Instagram, and Snapchat messages between me and Alex increase. I have no idea what I'm doing, but I do not feel scared.

I send her the book chapter about the dream, and she cries.

I have not cried in weeks.

I feel so connected to Alex, and I am not sure why.

Perhaps the gender dysphoria and brain cancer bring us together. Neither of us trust our bodies; neither of us trust what we have been given.

west virginia

I meet with Jodi, one of my best friends from high school, at the Pizza House in my hometown. I have not seen Jodi for about a year; I try to meet up with her every Christmas, but I am three months behind.

She brings all four yearbooks, prom pictures, and some sort of homecoming picture book that I did not know existed. We leaf through the yearbooks and Jodi marvels at how thin she was. She still seems thin to me. I do not remember half of the people in my graduating class, even though it was small. I don't know if this memory problem is from the acquired brain damage, or if I would have forgotten these people anyway.

You'll never guess who I am going to see! Jodi says.

Justin Timberlake.

I'm so excited, she says. *I've seen him twice now, and I know this time will be even better.*

In high school, Jodi was obsessed with the band NSYNC. She especially loved Lance Bass, who later came out as gay, just as a handful of her ex-boyfriends did.

I didn't have good luck with high school boyfriends, did I? Jodi says. *They were either gay or cheated on me.*

I'm so glad you found Doug, I say.

Me, too, she says. *You wouldn't believe how smart and funny my kids are. Brylee and Brody are both in the gifted program. They are going to transfer to a Christian school next year. Brylee just talks all the time. I have no idea where she gets that from!*

I love Jodi.

She is herself and nothing more or less.

Our server, Jamie, is another friend from high school. We take a picture together before we leave. As I'm grabbing my to-go cup, I clutch the Styrofoam too hard and the cup bursts all over the clean restaurant floor in an aneurysm of unsweetened tea.

I feel clumsy and terrible.

I cannot stop apologizing.

It's okay, sweetheart, Jamie tells me as she mops up my mess. *Just don't fall.*

Jamie grabs me a new drink. Jodi refuses to let me leave the restaurant without holding on to her arm.

You forget I work in healthcare, Suzi, she says.

No one has called me that since high school.

Jodi pulls her vehicle around, and I manage to pull myself into the beast. Jodi lives in the country and works as an X-ray technician; she needs this type of car to even leave her driveway in the snow.

We are old, but not that old.

She knows I am going to die.

I can tell by the way she helps me out of the car and into my parents' house.

west virginia

I am struck by how similar I am to my father. We hate tomatoes. We prefer to look at birds and squirrels and deer instead of talking. We cannot sit still for longer than ten seconds at a time. We both drive my mother crazy. He loves his cat, Princess Peppermint, more than any person. Lyme Disease made the left side of his brain swell, and he still has trouble walking.

Sometimes I do too.

nowhere

Terminal cancer makes everyone your best friend. I try to remember whom I spent my time with, whom I messaged, whom I talked to, before this shit started. I can count those people on one hand. Now I am expected to respond to everyone, to put on my *beautiful smile*, to pretend as if I am going to be okay just so everyone else can feel better about their own lives.

west virginia

My sister is on another bender. She calls me at 4:03 a.m. I do not hear the phone, and I do not answer.

She makes the following cryptic Facebook post:

Not everyone understands my lifestyle. Not everyone understands conspiracy theories. Sometimes I just want to throw myself into the void and see what happens next.

Is this because I did not answer the phone?

4:14 a.m.

I was asleep.

One of the symptoms of impending death is the inability to stay awake for more than a few hours at a time.

Part of me wonders if I am already gone.

nowhere

JC texts me screenshots of the messages between her and her ex-wife. The messages are snarky, passive aggressive. *If you want to file these divorce papers, this is how this needs to be done.*

They aren't even notarized. They won't hold up in court.

We are filing in BC. This is how it works.

These papers look worse than a sociology paper.

Sting.

JC's ex is a sociology professor, so this was a poisoned arrow.

I start to cry.

I feel sorry for JC. I do. I wish I could make things better for her. But the other part of me wants to grab her perfectly-angled shoulders and shake her until she stops feeling sorry for herself.

A small part of me wishes I had someone to argue with the way JC argues with her ex-wife. There is hatred, but there is passion. There is furious love. There is depth.

I have none of that with no one.

I am simply just dying alone, quietly and sadly.

boone, north carolina

When I am at my apartment alone, finally alone, really alone, I begin to organize and clean. The way I like it, not the way everyone else thinks it should be.

I find strands of long hair in a forgotten corner.

I am not sure if the hair is mine or JC's.

I want to cry but throw away the hair instead.

boone, north carolina

I always pictured a car crash.

My sister is not the worst driver ever.

I am the worst driver ever.

I would be checking my phone or trying to give an insulin shot or staring into the North Carolina forests as they whirled by in a mixture of dark and olive greens, and I would not notice that my tiny Scion had come upon a semi. I would crash into the back of the semi. My car would spin like an unsteady ballerina and roll into a creek bed on a road with no guard rail.

I would be going to Asheville to do something stupid with my cousin

Kyle and his wife Kelly, and my neck would break before anyone could find me and call 911. There wouldn't be service when they would try to call, and I would perish before any emergency personnel could find me and save me.

That's how I pictured death.

Or maybe I would be driving under a bridge that would collapse. I would suffocate with tons of concrete on my lungs and heart. My car would be nothing more than a flat piece of metal, and I would ascend into the universe with a purpose, with a meaning.

I did not picture death like this.

Sitting on a futon, bald and cold.

Nauseous and weak, watching snowbirds.

Tired and numb, listening to *Family Feud* on the television in my bedroom.

Wondering if I should pick up my old iced tea cups or just leave them to rot like my brain.

This type of death is removed.

I have nothing to do with explosions, nothing to do with the great beyond. I am small, I am weak, I am too nauseated to move, and I am too tired to feel that nausea.

Nausea. What a strange word.

I touch my head.

I am fucked.

I am so fucked.

I am so fucking fucked.

I do not know exactly when I will die. No one does. But there will be clear symptoms.

I will never be in remission.

Glioblastomas are incurable.

I am a 36-year-old female with a perfect pulse. Perfect temperature. Perfect blood pressure.

I am vital.

I am alive.

But not for long.

I will wet the bed, the internet says. I will shit my pants. I will talk of vacations, of packing my bags and *getting the fuck out of town.*

My apartment goes on the market the day after I finish treatment. This is a sign, I think, a sign of things to come.

boone, north carolina

I remember before I returned to Boone after visiting my parents, I was sitting with my father on the couch. He was watching an old John Wayne Western from 1934. Wild horses scattered and gunshots rang throughout the dusty, briar-filled valleys. Men fell off their horses, and horses tripped over invisible rocks.

These are something else, my dad said, and I had to agree. *Notice there's no music or anything. Just guys riding horses and shooting guns.*

I do not think I will get back on the horse.

boone, north carolina

This time last year, I was skating at a roller derby tournament in Texas. We won three of our four bouts; all of the games were close, and we were not expected to win any of them.

This year, I am crashed on my bathroom floor.

I was trying to put on a pair of pants, and I fell.

I hit my face on the corner of a suitcase.

I slam my hip into a book, and I have bruises that rival the one on my chest I got when an opposing derby player popped me with her shoulder.

I am not that heavy, but it takes me twenty minutes to lift myself from the floor.

I am screaming and crying and I do not know if it is from fear or pain.

nowhere

I remember seeing this photo by a famous photographer. He took a picture of his father who died the next day. His father had cancer, of course. In the photograph, he father reclines on a couch. The father is mostly bald and wears an old flannel. He watches television, and he is surrounded by old cups and empty snack cake wrappers.

This is the most realistic photograph I have ever seen.

This is how it will happen, I think. This is how I will go.

Quietly and softly.

I touch my head.

Everything hurts.

I have plans to see Alex at the end of April.

I sleep for sixteen hours a day.

There is no resolution.

I am fucked.

I am so fucked.

nowhere

If I returned to my hypothetical Victorian phrenologist's office, would she suggest hemp oil? Feel the bumps around my nicely-shaped skull and profess that I am cured?

It is highly unlikely.

After all, the phrenologist would want me to come back. She would want me to continue seeking her guidance, continue selling me hemp oil (and add frankincense to my bill next time,) continue paying her to discover my past, future, and current ailments.

Most of my friends are mad at me. I forget to return texts, I cannot keep up with their lives, and I call them out on their bullshit. (Reasoning, judgment, planning.)

I cannot remember what I ate for lunch yesterday. (Reflective faculties.)

Everything feels like a new normal. Everything feels like a cliché. (Time, associations, connections.)

The phrenologist would take all my money.

She would have no choice.

There is no cure.

I don't feel sick I don't feel sick I don't feel sick.

afterword by the writer's sister

Let me start by writing that just because your sister has cancer doesn't mean she is incapable of throwing keys at your face.

I was very worried about this happening.

I had one job.

I was summoned to be the chauffeur for my sister during her radiation treatments. No matter what she says, this is a job I did not take lightly.

As you read, I bought a special driving hat. One, to lighten the mood and two, to help me stay focused on the road. No matter what my sister wrote, I am not *the worst driver ever*, and I wanted to prove that.

I feel like I have always been the comedic relief in the family, but this time, I had the most important job.

The most precious cargo.

(She told me that was a cliché, but whatever. I like it.)

I don't know if she showed more bravery during her treatments or each time she got in the car with me. For her to go through all that and survive, the pressure was really on me to avoid roadkill squirrels, etc.

We had a few good runs from Boone to The Dash until one day the tires started wobbling and drowning out whatever Ben Folds song we had blasting in her tiny car that looks more like a roller skate than a vehicle.

Then it happened.

I was ruining everything.

Luckily, I have always been a fast reactor, so I immediately slowed down and pulled the large roller skate to the shoulder. The left front tire shot to the side of the highway and landed in the great beyond. I turned off the car, and my sister yanked the keys from the ignition.

Argument ensued.

I think we were both just fighting over neither one of us knowing what to do.

I just kept thinking, *You can't be angry with her! She has brain cancer for Christ sake!"*

I sat on the guardrail and smoked a cig to calm myself while my sister called her insurance company to request a tow. Highway patrol stopped by and returned the missing tire's hubcap.

We really needed it at that point.

He knew better than to ask too many questions.

After sitting for a few hours in a hillbilly tire shop in the middle-of-nowhere, all was well.

Although she never threw the keys in my face, I could sense the contemplation in her eyes during the peak of panic.

I guess what I'm trying to say is no matter her diagnosis, we will always be sisters. We will always argue, and ten minutes later, we will always be fine.

Because that's how it's always been, and that's how it will always be.

Suzanne Samples, Author

Suzanne teaches English at Appalachian State University in Boone, North Carolina. She was diagnosed with a frontal lobe glioblastoma multiforme at 36. She loves roller derby and lives on the side of a mountain with her pets Gatsby, Prufrock, and Duffles.

Barbara Lockwood, Editor

After leaving a satisfying career in medicine, Barbara Lockwood embraced her love of the well-written narrative and joined Running Wild Press to help their amazing authors birth their books and send them out into the world. She lives with her husband, cat, and bunny in a reconstructed church in the boondocks.

Acknowledgments

Suzanne would like to thank Lisa, Barbara, and the Running Wild team; her parents, Ted and Jenifer; her sister Sarah and their cousins Emily, Kyle, Megan, and Cathleen; her friend Shaina Crump for early edits of the manuscript; her friends Jenna, Jenn, Nodya, David, Julia, Kate, Cole, Gail, Amanda L., Amanda M., Hailie, Emily W., Michaela, Vanessa, Lisa, Jessica, Kelly B., Betsy, Amy, Travis, Rider, Sarah P., Kimberly, Rachel, Gabe, Crystal, Sarah W., Anthony, Mallory, David, Billie Jo, Suzette, Carrie, Bree, Lindsay, Lauren, and Jodi; her care team at Wake Forest Baptist Health; her teammates at Appalachian Roller Derby; and, of course, Ninja.

Past Titles

Running Wild Stories Anthology, Volume 1

Running Wild Anthology of Novellas, Volume 1

Jersey Diner by Lisa Diane Kastner

Magic Forgotten by Jack Hillman

The Kidnapped by Dwight L. Wilson

Running Wild Stories Anthology, Volume 2, Part 1

Running Wild's Best of 2017, AWP Special Edition

Build Your Music Career From Scratch, Second Edition by Andrae Alexander

Writers Resist: Anthology 2018 with featured editors Sara Marchant and Kit-Bacon Gressitt

Magic Forbidden by Jack Hillman

Upcoming Titles

Running Wild Stories Anthology, Volume 3

Dark Corners by Reuben Tihi Hayslett

Open My Eyes by Thomas Hahn

Running Wild Press publishes stories that cross genres with great stories and writing. Our team consists of:

Lisa Diane Kastner, Founder and Executive Editor
Jenna Faccenda, Public Relations
Rachael Angelo, Public Relations and Marketing
Tone Milazzo, Podcast Interviewer Extraordinnaire
Amrita Raman, Project Manager
Lisa Montagne, Director of Education
Barbara Lockwood, Editor
Cecile Serruf, Editor

Learn more about us and our stories at www.runningwildpress.com

Loved this story and want more? Follow us at
www.runningwildpress.com, www.facebook.com/runningwildpress, on
Twitter @lisadkastner @JadeBlackwater @RunWildBooks

CPSIA information can be obtained
at www.ICGtesting.com
Printed in the USA
LVHW041431160919
631221LV00012B/556/P